My Life in
Reflection

101 Poems
of
Love, War, Satire & Death

E. Tayloe Wise

Fiesta
PUBLISHING

My Life in Reflection: 101 Poems of Love, War, Satire & Death

ISBN: 979-8-9857477-7-5 (Paperback)

Library of Congress Control Number: 2022916405

Author: E. Tayloe Wise
Editor: Ashley Niro
Cover and Interior Design: Creative Instincts

First printing edition 2023

Printed in the United States of America.

10 9 8 7 6 5 4 3 2 1

Fiesta Publishing
PO Box 44984
Phoenix, AZ 85064

www.fiestapublishing.com

Table of Contents

To the Lonely Hearted – There Is Hope!
And Donna - You Know Why.

Foreword

The following poems were written over the past sixty years and contain my version of personal lifelong experiences and encounters. As a lover of poetry for most of my life, certain poets have inspired me. Two of the poems in this book are the style of Thomas Gray's, *Elegy Written in a Country Churchyard*, and Alfred Noyes', *The Highwayman*. Another poem is written in the style of Alexander Pope's, *The Rape of the Lock*. You will find some of the poems amusing, while others are whimsical. A few observe nature and the world in which we live, some are somewhat religious, while others are dark in their outlook on life. Poems of personal heartbreak, suffering, and betrayal are included, as well as my combat experiences in Vietnam and how that war tore our country apart in the 1960s-1970s and affected my outlook on life.

The majority of my poetry is dark — some may even say morbid — or incredibly irreligious. Many relate tragic stories and others contain evil in the form of Satan or other horrifying imaginary beasts from Hell that touch on the dark side of my erratic, convoluted view of the world. Incorporated in this book is my life as I have experienced it for more than sixty years.

Why such a dim view of life? For most of my life, I have been skating along the edge of a looming darkness as it advances like a dark shroud over the world. One will read in the following writings that most of my life has been one of seeing the glass as half empty, which reflects the futility I have seen, experienced, and endured for many years. Living with depression for much of my lifespan certainly hasn't helped matters, nor did my combat experiences in Vietnam. The lows of my life were certainly a trigger for the darkness that continues to permeate me. The result is an inner loneliness that constantly sits on my shoulder and is thus reflected in my poetry.

I have divided the following poetry into eight sections so that similar poems can be read together — Nature; Amusement, Life, Plus Odds & Ends; Ballads & Epics; two separate chapters about Loss & Lost Love; Mind Dreams; The Vietnam War; and Death.

For each of the chapters, a brief, explanatory comment of my thoughts concerning the section is included. Some of the poems have a comment added at the end to clarify, or comment upon, the genesis of that particular poem. Except for well-known public individuals and those who are now deceased, the name of each specific person mentioned in of these poems has been changed to a pseudonym or initials.

I hope you will find these poems interesting, informative, and thought-provoking.

Chapter 1
NATURE

Nature, whether it be a season, a wild animal, an insect, rain, flowers, or everyday things in our lives, has been an inspiration in my poetry.

** Previously published in *The Other Side: Mist, Mirrors & Strange Tales*. Phoenix, AZ: Fiesta Publishing, 2022. Used with the author's permission.

LIGHT

As the Last Beam of Receding Light
Shines Forth across the Hill
I Turn and Look at the Coming Night -
Which Steals Forth Steadily and Silently
To Catch That Last Glimmer of Light

Blackness Covers All and Is Inky Black
Dark - - Yes - - Likened unto DEATH -
Who Is the Evil Destroyer of Us All -
It Creeps in Quickly and Silently

From under Her Misty Veil
DIANA Looks Forth
And Views the Black Mantle
Creeping on Tiptoe over the Hill
Beauty - That Is the Word for Her
Over All She Watches and Protects
Truly, She Alone, Guards Us

Like a Babe in the Cradle -
She Cares for Us
Toward the Reddish-Yellow East I Now Turn -
As AURORA Spreads Her Misty Dawn
The Handsome, Yet Beautiful, APOLLO Approaches -
I See Him Weep Tears of Joy -
I Rejoice and Thank Him for Sparing Me

DAWN Is Gone Now -
The Sun in All His Covers Comes -
So Radiant . . . So Powerfully Strong!
I Look upon His Bright Yellow Colors and Know -
He Is Here, and DEATH Is Now Banished

We All Must Turn Now and Look -
Look? Where? To Heaven!
God Is Our Savior, Look to **HIM**
Truly, We All Must Realize
That without **HIM**
We Could Not Survive by Ourselves on Earth
Look to **HIM - HE** is Your Guiding Light

Give Thanks and Be Eternally Thankful
For **HE** Watches over You -
As a Shepherd Does His Sheep.

This was the first poem I wrote during the Spring of 1962.

SPRING

As I Sat in the Park One Day
In the Coolness of the Shade -
I Watched the Children Playing
Mothers Knitting, Old Men Sleeping
And I Thought to Myself
How Calm . . .
How Quaint . . .
How Beautiful . . .
This All Is

The Squirrels Are Hopping About
And the Pigeons Strutting Up and Down
They Are Tame -
Not Wild -
Like Some I Know Of -
The Sun Filters Through
The Newly Formed Leaves
In the Trees
I Look upon This Scene of Beauty -
And Greenness

How Beautiful
I Wish It Was Always Thus
In the Days of the Newborn Spring!

TO A SPIDER #1

Oh, Poor Wicked Thing -
Why Crawl You So upon the Ceiling?
You Go You Know Where
Yet on You Crawl!
Why?
Can You Stop Your Work?
Can You Tell Me?
You Live and Know Nothing -
Yet You Spin Your Endless Web
From Corner to Corner
From Wall to Wall
You Spin Your Fine Shiny Thread
Yet on You Crawl -
You Crawl across the Ceiling -
You Crawl down the Wall - -
You Crawl across the Floor - - -
Crawl On for All You May!
I Don't Care
I Just Watch You Go
Crawl On You Poor Wicked Animal!
Where E'er You May Go
You Care Not
Nor Do I.

TO A SPIDER #2

He Works His Wicked Web upon the Wall
Spinning and Spinning -
NEVER Ending -
NEVER Ceasing for One Second -
His Wily Tricks to Perform
As He Watches for the Wandering Wayfarer
He Waits -
To Listen -
And Nearby He Spies His Victim
Flying Freely through the Fair Air
To Be Caught in His Crooked Crag
Of Silver Gossamer Thread
The Little Fly Lightly Lands upon a Limb -
With Sleepy Eyes the Spider Spots Him Soon
And Climbs to Close His Clever Trap
The Frightened Fly Flees from the Fiend
But - -
In Its Confusion Flies
Directly into the Intricate Thread -
Interwoven - - Invisible
He Soars, And -
The Planned Plot Places Itself upon Him
Struggling - He Strives to Break the Web's
Voracious and Unending Grasp
While the Black Hairy Monster
Happily Marches

To His Next Meal
He Is No Horrible Heathen Here
The Meal Was Delicious
The Taste - Better!
So Life Must Depart
And Leave This Little World
For Death and the Daring Devil.

This poem was inspired by a drop of water on the pavement that looked like a spider.

A LIGHT

I See a Light Shining Way Off
It Is as Bright as a Guide
I Stumble toward It, But -
Lo! It Comes towards Me!
Take Me Quickly from This Spot!
No! No!! No!!!
Here It Comes!!!
Brighter and BRIGHTER!
I Cover My Eyes -
So Bright Is It
All of a Sudden It Is Misty
And the Light in Human Form
Shines Forth!
A Voice Has Spoken to Me - -

Now, As I Lie upon the Steep Crag
And Ponder - -
I Know! I Know the Light!
Yes, It Can but Be Only One Thing - -
God Has Spoken - So Let It Be
Depart I Now from This Sacred Place.

SLEEP

It Is Getting Foggy - So Foggy
I Can No Longer See Clearly
As My Eyes Close Off and On

You Cannot Fight It!
No - You Can't!
No Matter How Hard You Fight
It Will Take You

Take Me? Where?
To the Land of Nod
Yes - - It Is the One
Now Sleep - - Take Me!

THE RAIN

The Rain Comes Down on Little Feet
But - Who Does It Meet?
The Warm Mother Earth
It Covers with Its Mists
And It Has a Cloud of Thunder -
And Mirth
That Covers the Earth like a Shroud
The Clouds Move across the Sky Silently
And Strike without Warning
Rain Chooses Its Victims Blindly
Without Preference

In the Early Morning
The Rain Soaks the Ground
And Floods and Engulfs the Land
While It Sinks in All Around
It Is Always in Demand
For Everyone Desires Its Coolness
But Fears Its Mighty Power
It Flows Abundantly
Spreading across the Land
Making Man Cower

He Shudders in His Neolithic Cave
And Eyes the Approach of the Sun
He Runs into the Nave

To Find Comfort in the Sun -
But - the Sun Cannot Help Him
NEVER Will It Aid Man -
For the Future Is Dim
NEVER Will the Rain Lift Its Ban
Man Can Plead and Beg -
But the Rain Still Must Fall.

YESTERDAY, TOMORROW, AND TODAY

I Saw a Falling Star Today -
It Was Not Far Away
I Reached Out to Touch It
And Do Not Know What Became of It
All Bright and Shiny It Was -
Like It Always Does
The Tail So Brilliant with Light -
It Put Me All in a Fright
So Long! So Clear!! So Tranquil!!!
It Made Me Just So Restful -
I Leaned Back upon My Grassy Couch
And Rested Quietly in a Slouch
I Closed My Eyes to Think
But a Butterfly Made Them Blink
At Last, I Closed My Eyes in Peace
And Thought Not of That Dark Beast
Who Will Come to Carry All of Us Away -
Yesterday, Tomorrow, and Today
Round about You
It Wraps Its Octopus-Like Arms
And Takes You from All Life's Harms
I Shall Meet It Calmly -
Most Will Meet It Fearfully
So, Gladly Will I Rise

As Each New Day Dies
I Will Walk into a World of Hate
With Love as My Mate
So Fades the Falling Star -
My Life It Will Not Mar
The World Is Full of Blindness
So, I Will Bring It Kindness
The Dark Beast Can NEVER Bother Me
I Care Not for He
I Tread upon the World's Dirt
No Man Can I Hurt
I Throw Away My Cares
Because I Don't Like Men's Stares
They Hurt Me Not at All
Only Shroud That Final Pall
Now down the Hall of Life
I Tread with Love as My Wife
That Is - If I May -
Yesterday, Tomorrow, and Today.

THE FADING LIGHT

The Well Is Deep and Wide -
It Has No Sides -
And You, My Friend, Are in It
You Are Fit -
To End Up in Trouble
So Now Pops the Bubble -
Doom Will Pounce on Ye -
And You Shall NEVER Be Free
It Moves in Mysterious Ways -
Truly, There Are No Days -
The Black Dark Cloak Creeps In
Throughout the Green Fen
It Sweeps In o'er the Land
As Does the Flow of the Rio Grande
Taking Everything with It
At Nothing Will It Quit -
It Strikes on Time
Because It Is NEVER Blind
And You, My Friend, Are Caught
Just like a Rat You Thought -
There Is but One Fate
And You Are the Bait!
NEVER Forget the Dark Cloud -
Because It Is Your Shroud!
You Are Free Now -

And, Oh My Goodness How
The Sun Rises in the East
As Bread Does of Yeast
But It All Ends My Friend
As Does the Dying Night Wind
And That Calmness Lingers
As Doth the Ray-Like Fingers
Of the Fading Sunset.

THE LOYALTY OF A PET

There Is Something Sad
About a Man
Who Has Lost His Pet.
Have You Ever Looked
Into His Eyes?
Have You Seen the Raw Despair?
Have You Seen the Incredible Loneliness?
It's All There.
The Tragedy of It All
Is That Nothing Can Ever Replace
The Heartache.
The Loyalty of a Dog
Is Not Something to Be Forgotten.
Its Faithfulness Is Greater
Than That Which -
Many a Husband and Wife Have.
In Both Man and Dog
Existed a Bond of Indisputable Trust -
An Alliance So Strong
That When Severed by Death,
Is More Heart-Rendering Than
The Wildest Dreams.
Overcome by Emotion
The Man May Weep More
Than for One of His Own Kind.

And So, with His Heartbreaking Loss
He forlornly Trudges Along.
With the Memory Etched in His Eyes -
And His Sadness So Visible.
Now, There Is No Dog to Follow -
Or Pet -
Only a Beautiful Memory.

This poem is dedicated to all the dogs (and one cat!) who have graced my life and have been my lifelong pets — Blacky, Tar Baby, Brandy, Kahlua, Rusty, Cutty, Whiskey, Candy, Lady, Daly, and Stretch. God bless you all. RIP and know you all were dearly loved. I will see each of you when I cross the Rainbow Bridge.

FOOTPRINTS IN THE SAND

A Thousand Footprints in the Sand
Are All Washed Away,
And No One Really Knows
Who Stood There Before
Watching the Sea Recede?
Only the Sand Knows -
For It Felt Their Step
And Then, with Water,
Washed Itself Flat Again.
Caesar, Maybe, Stood Here -
But He Is Gone,
And So Are His Footprints,
And the Footprints of All Other Men
Who Stood and Watched the Sea
Break upon the Shore.

Footprints in the Sand
Stay a While and Go -
Let the Roar of the Sea,
And the Crash of Waves
Wash the Sand Free Again -
Cover and Smooth It Out
For Some Other Man
To Make Footprints in the Sand.

COME, PICK THE FLOWERS

Come Quickly My Friends to the Fields
And Pick the Flowers at Their Ends
Gather Them - Sniff Them - Keep Them.

The Sun Shines Sweetly on Their Beauty
The Clouds Quietly Cover Their Upturned Faces
Which Droop - Wither - and Die.

The Rain Pounds Down upon Them
While Winds Forcefully Bend Their Backs
The Silent Cold Quickly Chokes Their Life.

They Drop - Decay - and Disappear
The Leaves of Autumn Fall Here
The Earth - Thus Naked - Lies Barren.

Pretty Spring in Beauty Now Approaches
Making Earth Lie Pregnant with Seed
We See the Flowers Born Again.

Come Quickly My Friends into the Fields
Pick Them - Pluck Them - Keep Them
Save Them - - For Beauty Fades Quickly.

THE WOLF AND THE HARE

His Long Red Tongue
Hangs Down
As He Snarls and Slinks
Across the Snow
Slipping and Sliding
As He Stealthily
Strives to Survey
His Already Suspicious Prey
Which Crouches in Fear
As the Crunch of Padded -
No - - - Dreaded and Stealthy
Footsteps Approach

Cowering in the Chilly Air
He Skillfully Blends
Into the Shiny White Snow
As the Suspicious Wolf
Creeps Covertly Close
And with a Dash
He Bounds Off
With the Salivating Wolf
Not Far Behind -
Leaping and Bounding
He Eludes His Lupine Pursuer

Who Flounders in the Snow -
And its Deep Drifts
Before off it Balefully Creeps
To Wait and Try Another Day.

Chapter 2

AMUSEMENT, LIFE, PLUS ODDS & ENDS

Although much of my poetry is somewhat on the dark side, I did find time to write a few amusing and whimsical poems. The poetry in this chapter, *Amusement, Life, Plus Odds & Ends*, details ordinary and daily life and is a commentary on mundane occurrences that one encounters.

** Previously published in *The Other Side: Mist, Mirrors & Strange Tales*. Phoenix, AZ: Fiesta Publishing, 2022. Used with the author's permission.

TRAFFIC JAMS

The Traffic is Horrible -
A Tangle of Everything -
That NEVER Untangles!

Oh Stop!
Cease Will You?
No - NEVER!
Car upon Car -
Jamming Brakes and Honking Horns!
They Fill the Exhaust-Fumed Air!

NEVER! No Quiet!
Screech! A Tire Skids -
Maddened Drivers -
Pound Their NEVER Quiet Horns
In Frustration!

The Noise -
INTOLERABLE!!!
NEVER Ceasing Will It?
The World Must Take -
And Bear it All
O, Will You NEVER Cease, Traffic Jams?

WAITING

Here I am – Waiting
I'm Waiting –
For the Cursed Blackbird
He will Come –
For I am Waiting – Waiting

I am Waiting – Waiting
Waiting for the Chance –
To Kill That Double-Crosser!

I am Waiting – Waiting
He Thinks He's Tricky –
But NO!
I will get Him, For –

I am Waiting – Waiting
Waiting to Kill Him
Leave Me Now, For –
I am Waiting – Waiting!

GROSS, NASTY, WEIRD, HORRIBLE, VILE ANIMAL

When I See That Mass -
Of Protoplasmic Fat
Waddling along the Pavement
I Stop and Think -
What can it Be?
A John, Jim, or George?
It Looks like an Oversized Baboon -
Poor Corpulent Nasty Thing!
NO!
It's A Gross, Nasty, Weird, Horrible, Vile -
Animal!

Those Pencil-Long Fingers
Can Overlap a Glass!
And When it Grabs You -
You Feel as if a Giant Squid
Has Encompassed You 'Round About!
Ugh! Horrible!! Disgusting!!!
Gross, Nasty, Weird, Horrible, Vile -
Animal!

Fat is Nothing to It -
It is so Grossly Obese That -
It Looks like a Pregnant Elephant!
Is There No Pity in Your Heart

To Reform?
You Say You Try - Ha!
Try -- to Put on Weight!
NOT to Lose It!
Gross, Nasty, Weird, Horrible, Vile -
Animal!

You are but Truly Enormous, You -
Gross, Nasty, Weird, Horrible, Vile -
Mass of Whale Blubber!

Oh, God, Free us from its Presence -
For, NEVER Does it Bathe -
Ugh!
You Can Smell it across the Room -
It's a Gross, Nasty, Weird, Horrible Vile -
Repulsive Smell!!

And When it Touches You -
(By Accident We Hope!)
The Horrible Smell Rubs Off -
On You!
UGH!!!

The Stink Repels Everyone - All!
Begone from Us! Quickly Now!
Gross, Nasty, Weird, Horrible, Vile -
Animal!

It is Even Grosser -
For, When it Runs on the Earth

My Life in Reflection

Even the very Soil Vibrates -
And Shakes!
That Gross Animal Pounds It
To Death!
Its Feet are Thin and Long -
Just like a Kangaroo's Feet -
(Excuse Me Kanga - No Offense Intended!)
Gross, Nasty, Weird, Horrible, Vile
Animal!

Please! Don't Step on Us!
Shutter, All You People!
Beware!
Of its Overly Huge Feet -
Or, You may be Next!
Oh, Gross, Nasty, Weird, Horrible, Vile
Animal -
Why Do You Exist?
Why? Why?? Why???

This poem was written while I was a student at a boy's prep school in Virginia in the early 1960s. One of my friends was not exactly hygienic in his daily ablutions, so I penned this descriptive poem of his physicality and habits.

THE BRIDGE

There is a Bridge
Across Some Far Distant River
It is a Bridge to Nowhere
Take It and You Will See
It Leads to the Beyond.

THE RICH MAN?

Look at You -
You Call Yourself a Man?
Yet Look at Where You Stand -
Yes, Look!
Is it on Top of the World -
Or, is it in the Disease-Ridden Jungles?
Where Do You Stand?
Oh, Perhaps, Here? Yes?
I See You -
Gaunt, Lean, Hungry -
You're Standing in the Debris -
Of what was a Magnificent Mansion -
Whose House could it Be?
Is it a Rich Man's - or, a Poor Man's?
Rich - of Course!
What Else?
You were That Rich Man
But, Oh, Look at you Now!
Poor, Hungry, Beggar of a Man -
Yes, You were a Rich Man Once
Yet, You Despised People -
You Spat on Them -
They were Your Puppets -
Now, Look at You!
What has Happened?

Has Your World Come to an End?
No, It Hasn't!
You Brought This upon Yourself -
Deny It!!! If you Can
You Rotten Scum!
UGH!
Filth!!
That's What You Are!
Pigs aren't Fit to Sleep with You -
Yes, Pigs!
You Lived in Corruption -
And Now You Pay!
You Pay the Price
Every Rich Man Pays
I See the Smoke -
Rising from the Rubble
Your House has Burned -
Yes, Burned!
All Your Possessions -
All Your Keepsakes -
All Your Money -
All Your Italian-Made Clothes -
All Your Fine Furniture -
All Your Memories of Sweet Days Gone By -
All - Yes All!! Are Now Gone!
You are Forsaken Now -
Call on God Rich Man -
Go ahead - Call on God!

He Will Have Pity -
Pity . . . Pity . . . Pity
Yes, He will have Pity
A Rich Man You are No Longer
Just as from the Womb -
You were Born Naked in This World -
So, You Now Face it Naked Again!
Leave Me Now Rich Man -
Your Dreams are Mine to Destroy!
Mine!
Because I Am -
The God of Destruction!
I Abhor the Rich Bourgeois!!!
Yes, Hate!
Destruction I am Called -
Destruction am I!
I Destroy Everything!
Everything You Hold Dear -
Yes, Rich Man You were in My Way!
I Teach Rich Men to be Humble -
Beware of Me Rich Man -
For I am the God of DESTRUCTION!!!

THE PERMANENCE OF LOVE

There is NO Permanence in Loving -
What We Love Today -
We May Hate Tomorrow!
And Our Love Today
May be Totally Different
And Changed by Tomorrow -
That which We Love Today
May be Unrecognizable by Tomorrow.

THERE IS A SHIP

There is a Ship
We must Catch
Else We make the Slip
And miss our Catch
The Mist Rises Early
As We Stumble Aboard
All Gruff and Surly
Cursing All - Including The Lord!
Aurora Brightly in the East Rises
And Lights the Azure Sky
As our Captain Surmises
How Fast will our Ship Fly -
To the Great Barrier Reef
Where Hard Work will Await
To Give us Toil and Grief -
At Laboring Long and Late
To Make a Profit - and a Dime -
To Feed our Wives and Children
In Every Reasonable Clime
Through Times Thick and Thin
Our Days will be Long
As All our Days have Been
But We work for a Song
To Feed our Kith and Kin
We are but Only Poor Fishermen -

Yet, We Must Live!!
And So, We'll Help You Friend -
And You'll See What the Sea Will Give -
Peace.

BOTTLE

Ah! Bottle!
Where You Been?
It Seems -
My Bosom Friend -
I Been Seachin' for Ya!
You Seem to Hide -
Yet Stand Still!
Hey! Jack! Don't Go Waaay!
I Need You -
'Ol Buddy Pal!
You Reassure Me -
You Comfort Me -
Ah, You make Me
Feel so Cozy!
I Glow Inside -
Feel Soooo Fuzzy Warm -
And - All Because of You -
Good 'Ol Jack Daniels!
You Make Me Forget!
Carry Me down the Lane
To the Harbor of Lethe -
Take My Pain -
My Sorrow - -
My Sadness - - -
Make Me Feel Real Good -

Again!!!
Ah! You're such a Peach!
You Taste so Delicious!!!
Can I Pleas' have some Mo'?
Ah, Yes! - That's Wonderful!
Feels Sooo Good!
Wish I had More -
But . . . Now You're Empty!
An' I'm Growing Drowsy -
Think I'll take a Snooze
And Wake Up -
To Drink More Booze!
Ah . . . Bottle -
I Luv Ya!!!
You're so Good -
To Me!
Can't Wait Til -
We Meet Again!
ZZZZZZZZZZZZZZ

D.'S PRAYER

Thank You for the Brightness
You have brought into My Life!
Even Tho' it may Only be Temporary -
I Still Thank You -
For That Wonderful Brilliance -
You Will NEVER Know -
How much your Presence
Has brought Great Joy to Me -
My Life has been so Cloudy . . .
These Last Few Months -
And Now, You have Provided Me -
With a Little Ray of Warm Sunshine
Which, I Hope, will Grow Larger -
The Joy of the Last Few Days -
Has been brought to Me
By Your Radiance -
Thank You for That Peace
Which My Mind Now Has -
I Hope and Fervently Pray
That I can also Bring -
The Same Gaiety -
And Light-Headedness -
Into your Life
As you have done for Mine!
I Pray That our Budding Friendship

May, in the Future, Prosper -
Thank You for Your Luminosity -
And the Sparkle in your Eyes -
May Peace of Mind and Joy
Be Ever with You -
And May your Ray of Sunshine
Shine upon Me and You
As Long As -
God Wills!
Amen!

This was written in 1973 for a woman named D., whom I had met. I have no idea of her last name or who exactly she was, but our budding relationship, as evidenced by this poem, must have been brief!

PEOPLE

People
Living Their Lives
In Little Boxes
Going from Day to Day -
To Point A -
To Point B - -
To Point C - - -
To Point D - - - -
NEVER Realizing
They're Trapped
Going from Corner to Corner
Doing the same Ol' Thing
Over and Over
Like Rats in a Labyrinth
Wake Up People!
There's a World out There!
There's a Life Outside!
Things to Do -
Things to See -
Can't You See?
Can't You Believe?
There's more out There
Than Just Your Little Box
A Whole Lot More -
So Much to Do -

So Much to See -
If . . . You Can Get Out
There's so much to Do
On the Outside!!
So Much! So Much!! So MUCH!!!
I Wonder Why I'm Inside?

THE BAR #1

Well, I Sipped
A Lot of Coffee -
And Eased Many a Beer
Down My Weary Old Dry Throat
While Sitting Alone
In a Multitude
Of Deserted Bars
Across This Land
Dotted across the Landscapes -
Of My Beer and Rum-Soaked Brain -
Are the Fears and Hopes -
Of Living Alone -
So, Here it Is -
Another Fucking Saturday Night -
And Here I Am -
As Usual!
At One of My Favorite Haunts!
A Friendly Watering Hole
Where the Barkeep -
Knows Me by Name -
And What I like to Drink -
Fingering My Long-Necked Bottle -
Of Golden Nectar -
Quenching My Parched Taste Buds -
Again -

Easing the Alcohol Down -
And Praying the Next Minute
Will Pass a Little More Speedily -
Because Going Home -
To an Empty House -
To an Empty Bed -
Without Someone
Eagerly Awaiting Your Return -
Is Absolutely NO Fun -
Living Alone without a Woman
To Hold -
To Snuggle - -
To Caress - - -
Is Incredibly Hurtful -
Watching the 6:30 News
On the Sports Bar's TV
I Think -
Thank God in a Few Hours -
It'll be Sunday -
And another Fucking Day
Will be Over -
Hey Bartender!!
Give Me Another -
It's for the Pain!

THE BAR #2

Well, Here I Am -
Sitting All Alone -
In my Neighborhood Bar -
Drinking Again!
The Single Life is Jus'
Not for Me -
Since You Left -
And I Jus' Can't Face
That Empty House -
Right Now

CHORUS

Lonely . . . Lonely . . . Lonely
God it's Hell -
Livin' Alone -
I'm an Empty Man -
Livin' an Empty Life -
Without You!

Well, Here I Am -
Drinkin' All My Sorrows Away -
Thinkin' 'bout You -
Wonderin' 'bout You -
Knowin' I Can't Ever -
Sleep with You beside Me -

Again!!!
'Cause it's Over!
Really . . . Really . . . Really . . .
Over!
You Found Another -
And Left Me for Him!

CHORUS

Lonely . . . Lonely . . . Lonely
God, it's Hell -
Livin' Alone -
I'm an Empty Man -
Livin' an Empty Life -
Without You!

Well, Here I Am -
Watching that Couple
In the Corner Booth -
Wishin' it was You and Me -
They Seem . . . So in Love -
An' I'm Crying so DAMN Hard -
Inside!!!
'Cause They Got Love -
And All I Got is Pain -
And an Awful Awful Lot -
Of Loneliness

CHORUS

Lonely . . . Lonely . . . Lonely
God it's Hell -
Livin' Alone -
I'm an Empty Man -
Livin' an Empty Life -
Without You!

Well, Here I Am
Starin' through the Barroom Window -
Watchin' Another Couple -
Pushin' a Baby Stroller -
Down the Street
He Looks at Her -
And She at Him -
With So Much Love -
In both Their Eyes
And My World's -
Comin' Apart!

CHORUS

Lonely . . . Lonely . . . Lonely
God it's Hell -
Livin' Alone -
I'm an Empty Man -
Livin' an Empty Life -
Without You!

Well, Here I Am -
Hey! Barkeep -
Hit Me Again!!
I Need the Courage -
To Go Back Home -
And Sleep Alone Again -
Another Night Without -
Her Loving Arms -
To Hold Me -
Touch Me - -
Love Me - - -

CHORUS

Lonely . . . Lonely . . . Lonely
God it's Hell -
Livin' Alone -
I'm an Empty Man -
Livin' an Empty Life -
Without You!

PRAYER

We Thank You for This Joyous Occasion -
And We Thank You for This Precious Moment
That You Have Given Each of Us -
In This Room -
Thank You for Making Us
The Lucky and Fortunate Ones
To Attend This Hour of Joy!
We Pray for Those not Here -
We Ask That You Bless US
And Those We Dearly Love -
Who also cannot be Here -
For Each and Every One of Us -
We Ask for You to Make Our World
A Better One!
We Pray That You bring Peace
To That World in which We Live.

FOLLY

Ah, to Dream -
Of What Might Have Been -
Instead of What Is -
Is Folly -
For What Might Have Been -
Is Only a Fantasy -
In the Mind's Eyes -
And Fantasy is Only -
A Step Away From
Pleasure . . . or Insanity.

THE OTHER WORLD

Our God Is Dead -
Yet Satan Still Lives -
Because Our World Died -
Women Are the World
And, For Me, the World -
Is Now Dead!
I Discovered My World -
On the OTHER SIDE!
In That Other Dimension
Coexistent with Ours
Here on Earth -
Parallel with Us -
Where, Many Times
I Have Been -
There Are Doors
Leading to It
Here and There -
Invisible . . . Yet Shimmering -
Which Stand Ajar -
Admitting Only
A Select Few -
The Evil That Lurks
Within Us All -
Chases Us from Our World -
Into the Next -

Some - A Few - of Us
Are Fortunate Enough
To Escape Into -
The Other World
We Step Thru the Opening -
Into That Shadow World,
And Escape at Last -
The Grim Reality of Our World!
We Flee the Rantings -
Of Madmen -
Who Profess to Know
What Is Really Best
For All Mankind -
Yet - I Warn You -
To Escape to That
Next Dimension
Is Like Suicide -
Once You Step Over -
Or Pull the Trigger -
There Is No Return Journey -
Sometimes I Wonder
Which World
Would Suit Me Best?
Is Leaving Really
So Selfish Then?
For . . . By Departing
I Make Myself Happy -
Yet, Others Would View It

As a Selfish Act -
But, One's Inner Peace
Is Destiny!
And DESTINY
Must Be Paramount -
Else We Kowtow
To the Whims of Others!
So -
One Day - -
Soon - - -
I Intend to Take
That Step
Into That Other Dimension -
The Other World -
Ah, It Will Be an Adventure
Won't It?

Chapter 3

BALLADS & EPICS

In my early days of composing poems, I penned some ballad-like poetry in the style of various poets whom I admired. I enjoyed the satire of *The Rape of the Lock* by Alexander Pope (1688-1744) and the romantically sad story related in *The Highwayman* by Alfred Noyes (1880-1958), which has always been my favorite poem.

** Previously published in *The Other Side: Mist, Mirrors & Strange Tales*. Phoenix, AZ: Fiesta Publishing, 2022. Used with the author's permission.

THE LITTLE VILLAGE COURTYARD

It was a Pale Dark Night That the Soldiers Came -
NEVER! NEVER!! NEVER!!!
To Return Again -
Tramp! Tramp!! Tramp!!!

The Long Forgotten March of One Hundred Men -
Who Came and Went to Fight for Their Kin
Yes, I Remember That Moon Clouded Night
As Men Proudly Marched
Across our Little Village Courtyard
I Stood at My Window -
And Watched the Shadows
Tramp! Tramp!! Tramp!!!

The Leather on Their Boots Worn -
Their Clothes, Soiled, Dirty, and Torn -
Yes, Dirty with the Mud of a Thousand Trenches -
Dirty with the Blood of Countless Men
Ragged and Torn were They
In a Horrible State of Mildew and Decay
Their Helmets Filled with Dents and Holes
Was the Scorn of These One Hundred Souls
Tramp! Tramp!! Tramp!!!

Their Heavy Panting and Breathing can be Heard
It comes from a Dog-Tired March across the Land
By the Order of some Unknown Command
Look at Their Faces My Children -
Those are the Faces of Wearied Men
Sweat Slides down a Dirty, Half-Shaven Face
Their Beards of many Days Drip
Grime, Dirt, and Sweat
Their Eyes are Bloodshot
And Their Mouths set Firm
There is No One Smiling among This Group -
Theirs is the Duty to Fight for Liberty and Freedom -
Freedom from the Hated Tyrant
Now, My People Turn Your Heads
And Look at Their Hands -
Dirty, Bloody, Scar-Ridden Hands -
This is the Finger That Pulls the Trigger
That Deadly Trigger Which Set Off This War!
Our Men Shall Stop It!
Tramp! Tramp!! Tramp!!!

They are almost Gone Now
From Our Little Village Courtyard -
One Hundred March Onward
The Front Line Scarce Fifteen Miles Beyond -
Trenches and Barb Wire and Breastworks Full -
The Toil of Sleepless Men -
Men who Lie in Dirty Water-Filled Trenches -
Some will lie There Forever!

Tramp! Tramp!! Tramp!!!
They go to Fight for What is Right
But is it Right?
This Horrible War – I Mean?
Now I Hear Their Muffled Footsteps Fade -
Yes, They are Gone - To Fight for Us!
Who Sit, Wait, Worry, and Watch
Tramp! Tramp!! Tramp!!!

The Little Village Courtyard is Left Behind -
Now No One Passes Through -
Perhaps NEVER Again will They Come -
Will They Ever Return -
To March Back over it Again?
Tell Me, Sir, Will They?
For Some Yes - For Others No
I Look upon the Dirty Cobblestones -
Cakes of Mud Fallen Off Here and There -
A Gust of Wind Picks up a Piece of Paper -
It is a Picture of a Winsome Girl -
Perhaps a Mother or a Loved One?
Boom! Boom!! Boom!!!

The Fierce Blast of the Far Distant Cannon is Heard -
Its Echoes Reverberate through our Square
It Pounds like the Mighty Heart
Which NEVER Stops -
Pound! Pound!! Pound!!! Pound!!!!

Oh, Will it NEVER Stop?
No - It Won't!
Until Every Man Dies -
Or, a New Front is Reached
The Night Darkens
And Still I Hear That Accursed Sound
I Sleep with It -
I Live with It -
Perhaps One Morning
I Shall Awake
And It Will be Gone
Gone, Yes! Like a Scary Dream
It Does! I Awake with the Dawn
It IS Gone!
I Look upon the Sun-Filled Courtyard
And Wonder - Who Today Will Cross It?
Then, I Hear That Dreadful Sound
Tramp! Tramp!! Tramp!!!

An Ominous Sound comes from the Front!
Have Our Men Won? – Or Lost?
Then I Know the Sad Answer -
The Bullet-Torn Ranks of our Soldiers Appear
As if God Sent Them back Here
No Longer the One Hundred -
Coats and Jackets are Torn
Men's Arms Hang in Bloody Slings -
And I Now see the Blood Marks of War
Faces - Sad and Dreary -

My Life in Reflection

No Sleep for the Walking Weary
Their Helmets Cocked to One Side or the Other -
The Snaps Swinging To and Fro
Some Stumble, Stagger, While Others Limp -
No More the Brave and Gallant One Hundred
Tramp! Tramp!! Tramp!!!

They Come and Go in small Groups -
There! A Soldier Stoops!
And Picks up His Long-Lost Beauty!
She's Mud-Stained Now
But He Places Her Nearest His Heart
Oh, Pitiful Sight!
Now My Eyes See Men -
On Stretchers, Crying, Weeping, Begging!
Damn the War - I Hate You!
Some Pause and Drink at the Fountain -
They Gulp the Bitter Water Down
And Wash Their Muddy Hands and Faces
Some Linger . . . Then Resume the March -
Where Will They Go?
Some Calmly Fill Their Empty Canteens -
Others Rush
Suddenly - A Man Drops
Falls like a Brick upon the Cobblestones
A Comrade Prods Him with a Foot -
Too Late! . . . He's Dead!
Tramp! Tramp!! Tramp!!!

The Courtyard Square Stands Empty Now -
No More Men Will Cross it with Bowed Heads -
The Invader Follows -
Yes! He comes to see What He has Done -
Hateful Tyrant!
Tramp! Tramp!! Tramp!!!
The Retreating Footsteps Fade
And Now, I Await the Invader -
The Courtyard Lies Empty
Here and There a Piece of Paper Wafts
And a Dead Man's Face -
Lies in the Cobblestone's Grooves
Not Far Away his Rifle Lies
NEVER again to be Touched by him at Sunrise
His Helmet Lies like an Overturned Turtle -
Rocking Back and Forth with the Wind -
Click! Click!! Click!!!

The Invader Enters the Mud-Filled Courtyard
Slowly He Looks Around
Until He Spies the Dead Man
Cautiously, like a Cat, He Inches Forward -
Warily He Circles His Prey -
Jabs the lifeless body with his Rifle Butt
Then Sticks Him with His Blood-Stained Bayonet
And Discerns the Man is Truly Dead
A Wicked Sneer of Glee crosses his Face
And He Wipes His Sweaty Forehead
Pow! Pow!! Pow!!!

My Life in Reflection

What has Happened?
Oh Look! Our Invader's Evil Smirk Changes -
Changes to One of Absolute Horror!
Grabbing His Belly -
He Crumples beside the Defender
Like a Wadded up Piece of Paper -
Hooray! The Invader Dies
Who fired those Shots?
Who could it Be?
Perhaps One of the Retreating Hundred?
Who Knows?
Click! Click!! Click!!!

The Invader's Goose-Stepping Clomp of Boots
Tells Me That His Regiment Approaches
Our Little Village Courtyard
Stands Bare before Him
Death to the Invader!
That Hateful Tyrant!
The Conqueror has Come -
When Will the One Hundred Return?
Tramp! Tramp!! Tramp!!!

THE COWBOY

The Gray Clouds Drifted Slowly
Across the Old Cowboy's Face -
Making it Difficult to See
It became Darker than a Black Ace

Bone-Tired, the Cowboy sat Silently
While His Horse Nibbled on the Sage Brush
He Dragged on His Cigarette Calmly
Letting Silence come to the Desert with a Hush

The Wind Blows Coolly from the East
Gathering the Dark Clouds in the Sky
So, Soon the Cowboy would Feast
On Riches - That Would Cause Him to Die

In the Brush a Coyote Scurried Stealthily Away
Perking up His Ears - The Horse Shied
And the Golden Sun's Last Ray
Faded Slowly into the Night and Died

The Hot Dusty Desert Cooled Quickly
When the East Wind Struck It
To Blow the Dirty Dust Haphazardly
As His Horse Chomped at its Bit

My Life in Reflection

Scarred by Time, Wind, and Rain -
The Cowboy's Face tells the Tale
Of many a Pain -
Out There on the Distant Trail

A Beard of a Week's Growth
Hid the Features of his Weary Face
Lightning Flashed - Startling Them Both
Making the Horse Pace

"Whoa Boy!" the Cowpoke Calmly Said
Soothing His Horse's Twisted Mane
To Stop the Frightened Hoof's Tread -
Tonight the Elements were not Sane

The Distant Sound of Thunder
Reached Their Ears
And Rolled on without a Blunder
Bringing Light . . . Rain . . . Tears

His Cigarette Now Finished
He Drops it to the Ground
The Thunder was far from Diminished
But Grew Louder in Sound -

The Rain Beat Down upon Him
Forcing Him to Button his Dusty Coat
Frayed, Worn, Ripped, and Colored Dim
Made from the Hide of a Goat

His Black Boots would hold up Well
But His Denims would Soak Through
Perhaps to send Him to Hell
With a Cold That would make Him Blue

The Storm, Then . . . in All its Fury
Lashed Them with its Rain and Wind
After This his Horse would be hard to Curry
But the Storm would not Bend

As Suddenly as it Came - The Tempest Abated
And Left Them Drenched -
All because He was Fated
Said the Fates to be Lynched

The Water Dripped off his Hat
As the Horse Shook to get Dry
And Nickered at a Low-Flying Bat
Which Gave Off a High-Pitched Cry

Sliding from his Saddle
The Cowboy stomped his Feet
To get Warm for the Forthcoming Battle
When the Forces of Evil would Meet.

An incomplete poem written in the Fall of 1963.

DEATH'S DARK COACHES COME MARCHING ON

The Laboring Swain Toils His Weary Way
Up the Long, Rock-Strewn Hill;
And Men of Honor Say
Its Soil Was Rich to Till.

High Up on That Promontory
He Sits Himself Slowly Down
To Ponder the Old Remembered Story
That for Years Went 'Round.

The God Zephyrus Sweetly Blows
As the Blood-Red Sun Slowly Sinks,
And His Tattered Clothes
To Sad Misfortune He Links.

O'er the Mountain in the West
Those Bright Rays Begin to Fade,
And the Swain Remembers That He Did His Best
As by God He Was Often Bade.

He Turns to View the Valley
Which Shadows of the Coming Night
Cover O'er the Lea,
And Silent Death Comes to Test His Fearful Might.

Some Mysterious Darkness Approaches,
Summoning His Pale White Sister - the Moon,
To Show the Way for Death's Dark Coaches
That Will Be Coming Soon.

From the Dark Forbidden Caves Emerge the Bats
To Herald the Near Advent of Mighty Death;
And from the Distant Swamp Rise Bothersome Gnats
To Fight Every Man's Breath.

Now Comes the Silent Fog
Which Covers the Moor
Rolling Silently O'er Many a Fallen Log,
And Obscuring Each Friendly Village Door.

To the Swain's Aged Eyes Come Tears
As He Gazed upon the Hamlet,
Where for Many Long-Ago Years
Love Had Run the Gauntlet.

Ah, Yes, the Old Man Remembers Well
The Sad Tale of Two Lovers
Upon Whose Lives the Axe of Death Fell
Like the Land Which the Falling Snow Covers.

Their Love Was Spoke of Afar;
A True Romance 'Twas in Every Way
To Be Sure Nothing Could Mar
The Vows to Be Spoken on That Future Day.

But, Oh Beware the Unseen
Which Lurks at Every Corner
With Two Evil Eyes That Gleam
On Every Mourner.

Spring Arrived at the Village in Full Bloom,
And the Man Picked Many a Flower
Not Suspecting the Forthcoming Doom
As He Walked Her Back to Her Bower.

With Flowers Came Love Unending
And Every Good Night Kiss
Was Like Love Fully Blending
Each Time They Parted from Their Happy Bliss.

When They Strolled Around the Village Square
The Children Played as the Old Surveyed,
And She Plaited Long Love Knots in Her Hair
Walking in Pastures Where the Horses Neighed.

Many a Stroll They Took upon the Heath,
And Oftentimes They Rested by a Spring;
When (As Goes the Village Belief),
He Gave Her Their Engagement Ring.

The Story Was Oft Told
That, As They Rested by This Brook,
(Whose Sweet Waters Were Very Old)
They Gave Each Other Many a Loving Look.

As They Lay by That Slow Moving Stream
Squirrels and Birds Would Hop Around Them,
And They Were Kind to God's Lively Creatures - Not Mean
As Are Some Evil-Minded Men.

They Rested Here Very Often to Talk
Of Many Matters on Their Minds,
And No One in This Direction Would Walk
For Fear of Disturbing Such a Love That Binds.

It Was on Such Nights as This One
That Those Two Lovers Met at the Old Village Barn
To Talk of Love and Many Things They Had Done
While Listening to the Old Folks Spinning a Yarn.

For Love Is NEVER Lost
Tho' Lovers May Be Parted
On Seas That Are Tempest Tossed
Or on Lands Far from Each Departed.

The Man Was a Tall Strapping Youth
Who Worked at the Village Smithy;
And He NEVER Spoke an Unkind Word in Truth
To the One He Loved Who Was So Pretty.

He Loved Her with All His Heart,
And She with All of Hers Likewise.
Each Day He Met Her in the Village Mart
For, You See, Strong Love NEVER Dies.

My Life in Reflection

Oh, Sweet Love! How Long Do You Last?
Is It a Year . . . Month . . . Or Day
O'er Which Your Magic Spell Is Cast,
Or Does It Continue to the Last Words People Say?

She Was the Fairest Lass to Behold
Her Golden Hair Streamed Down Her Back,
And Her Face Was of Such a Beautiful Mold
That Not a Single Virtue Did She Lack.

All the Village Talked
Of the Day They Would Marry,
And Every Day in the Green Meadows They Walked
To Pass the Time and Tarry.

But Plans of Lovers by Unseen Hands Are Moved
And Evil Shall Step In
As Oft Has Been Proved;
And the Black Forces Will Not Stop Them.

Remembering These Long-Forgotten Facts
The Swain Looks Down
And Now Clearly Sees Death's Tracks
Engraved upon the Ground.

The Dark Vaults of His Memory Are Opened,
And Pages of Time Unroll
From the Day They Were Penned
Up in His Mind's Scroll.

On Their Wedding Day the Sun Was Bright,
And Many Flowers Were in Bloom
So That Spring Could Be Smelt Every Night
To Mark the Dread Approach of Gloom.

No Happier Couple Was There in All the Land
As They Stood on God's Holy Ground,
And When the Village Pastor Joined Them Hand in Hand
The Village's Gaiety Was a Sound.

A Marriage Feast Was Held Nearby,
And the Food Was Plentiful
So That before Night Was to Draw Nigh
Everyone Was to Partake a Delicious Mouthful.

A Town of Some Considerable Size
Lay Near This Happy Village Life,
And There Many a Villager Had Won a Prize
For the Goods Raised on His Fief.

In This Lovely Town
They Were to Spend Their Honeymoon,
And the Story Went 'Round
They Were to Leave Late That Afternoon.

Oh, These Poor Unsuspecting People!
Can No One See the Horrible Approach of Death
That Lurks Behind Every Steeple
To Worry Every Man's Breath?

My Life in Reflection

Why God Is Love to be So Short
That Was So Sweet?
As You Sit before That Great Judgment Court
Can You Not Stop Death So Fleet?

The Sun Has Headed to Bed
Before Dark Night Creeps Near;
And, As the Last Dying Rays Are Fled,
The Village Bids Adieu to the Lovers So Dear.

The Timely Coach Draws Up
Before the Village Inn Door
Where the Happy Couple Have Sup
So to Love Each Other More.

Hand in Hand the Ill-Fated Coach They Enter
As the Dark Mysterious
Prepares to Fully and Finally Splinter
This Wonderful Love So Glorious.

Not Many Miles Away
Lies Waiting in the Bush a Highwayman
Bent on Desire to Have Money That Day -
If - He Possibly Can.

The Coach master Drives His Horses Hard
For Coming Quickly Is an Inky Black Storm,
And, Now, Death Must Play His Final Card
According to Correct Form.

The Cold Rain Comes Pelting Down
While This Varlet Waits upon His Black Steed -
A Horse That Paws at the Muddy Ground
While His Master Waits to Commit This Heinous Deed.

Lightning Flashes Cover the Earth and Sky,
And It Seems Thor Is Displeased
And Throws His Yellow Bolts from on High
So, His Temper Will Be Appeased.

But God No Longer Controls the Situation
For Death Has Its Work Cut Out,
And No Man - in Whatever Station -
Can Stop This Bout.

Oh God - How Can You Be So Cruel
As to Let Death Separate This Pair?
She Is the Fairest Jewel
That Ever Breathed This Mortal Air!

The Love Story Now Unravels
As the Highwayman Hears the Horse's Tread
That along the Road Travels
Like Something from the Dead.

He Draws His Pistol Now
And Cocks It with Sureness
And Waits So Long He Knows Not How
'Til He Hears Nearby the Horse's Harness.

My Life in Reflection

Down He Rides upon the Stage
And Yells for the Driver
(A Man of Ancient Age)
To Stop or He'll Soon Be a Cadaver.

The Horses in the Coachman Quickly Reins -
For He Has No Wish to Die;
He'd Rather See This Rogue in Chains
Than from His Bullets Fly.

Dressed in Black the Robber Demands
All the Money the Travelers Own,
As Other Passengers Follow His Command;
The Lovers Are Left Alone.

The Devil Aims His Pistol
Straight at the Smith's Breast.
Soon Death's Bell Will Toll,
And Someone Will Be Laid to Rest.

Damn the Man Who'll Hurt the Innocent!
To Make a Few Pence Here and There,
Because He Thinks Life Isn't Worth a Cent;
And - That No One Will Care!

"Kind Sir," the Smith Begs, "Please Spare Us.
We Have So Little to Give
This Is Not Worth All This Fuss
For Which a Man, Like Yourself, Must Live."

"You Have 'Til the Count of Three
To Hand Over All You Possess,
Or Soon, from Life You'll Be Free
From My Bullet in Your Chest."

The Lover Would Not Budge
As the Rain Now Fell Like Stones,
And Thor Did Now Indulge
In Lightning Which Cracked in Somber Tones.

Aeolus Let Loose His Stormy Winds
Which Blew the Rain in Torrents,
But - Death Always Wins
Over All the Tears Man Vents.

The Nearby Trees Sway
As If Moved by Some Unknown Hand,
For There Is to Be a Death This Day
Which Will Be Mourned Throughout the Land.

From Out of All This Tumult
Comes a Sharp Pistol Crack.
The Rogue Has Committed a Heinous Fault
On this Damned Night So Black.

My Life in Reflection

The Elements Tried Their Best,
But Lo - What Is This Horrid Tragedy?
The One Who Was So Blest
Lies Now in Her Lover's Arms So Bloody!

Neither Wind, Nor Rain, Nor Lightning Could Defect
Black Death in His Planned Track
For She Had Leaped to Protect
Her Lover from the Bullet That Now Lodged in Her Back.

The Highwayman Has Seen His Mistake,
And He Stirs His Gallant Charger to Flee;
But No More Errors Will He Make;
The Lover Shoots Him Down with Avenging Glee.

Now, Suddenly Nature Ceases Her Violent Acts;
And the Lightning, Wind, and Rain Are Still
As Is a Virgin Forest before the First Settler's Axe,
Or after the Hunter Has Made His Kill.

He Clasps Her Tightly in the Cradle of His Massive Arm
But Life Ebbs from Her Pretty Lip;
For Death Has Done His Wicked and Evil Harm,
And No More Breaths of Air Will She Sip.

Her Eyes Are Seen to Flutter,
And Her Lips Move Convulsively
As If Some Words They Wish to Utter.
"I Loved You," She Said, "Faithfully."

What More Is There to Say?
For She Is Now Gone,
And He Took Her Body Back That Black Day
To Lament Her for O So Long!

Death Comes Silently Down Every Street
And Will Smile So Evilly
At Every Happy Soul He Will Meet
Tho' They Pass by Him Civilly.

"Aye, Well Remember I,"
Saith The Swain
As He Contemplates the Now Dawn-Colored Sky
And Silently Takes God's Name in Vain.

He Has Lived His Natural Span
Knowing and Hearing Many a Tale
While Wandering 'Round Earth's Land
Over Many a Hill and Dale.

The Swain's Old Ears Perk Up;
He Hears the Sound of Hoofs
That along the Ground Do Gallop
Sounding Like Rain Splattering on House Top Roofs.

Soon Aurora Unfolds Her Multi-Colored Dawn,
And Apollo Follows Not Far Behind.
To This Wind-Swept Place a Villager Is Drawn
To Search for One of His Own Kind.

My Life in Reflection

On the Hillside They Found the Swain's Body There
With a Face Now So Content,
They Bore His Body to the Village Square
Where His Homeward Steps Were So Often Bent.

They Buried Him in the Earthy Clay
To Sleep Peacefully in His Grave.
They Placed Him Not One Yard Away
From the Slain Girl to Whom His Love He Gave.

Oh, Love Is Sweet
And Love Is Kind;
But Death Will We Always Meet;
The Mortal Fear of Each Man's Mind.

So Was It When Life Started,
So Is It Now,
And Not One Fear Hath Departed
From Man's Eternal Brow.

This poem is written in the style of both Alfred Noyes' poem *The Highwayman* and Thomas Gray's *Elegy Written in a Country Churchyard*, and is dedicated to Ben F. Turner (RIP).

THE OGRE, PORGY, AND THE GHOUL (A SATIRICAL TRAGEDY)

CANTO I

An Ogre was Once on Our Earth
Who Ruled a Public High School with Mirth -
A Foxy Wife had He
Who went by the Name of Porgy -
A Teacher was She in Home Ec
And Children came at Her Every Beck
All Students were at The Ogre's Command
Such Ruled This Man!
Our School did Thrive in Harmonic Felicity -
No like School was There in All our City -
So, Now The Muse, Ben, I Invoke -
To Read these Words Herein Spoke -
Although I am no Fool!
I shall Write of the Fate of Our High School!

CANTO II

This Ogre - Indeed - Was a Horrible Man -
There Were None like Him in all Our Land -

My Life in Reflection

He had in his School Many Students
Not Well-Versed in Prudence
And Not a One did He Know by Face or Name -
Which Decreased his Fame -
This Man just Loved to Cuss
He Commanded Cursing be Spoken by All of Us -
Because He Delighted in Glee -
At such Language That was Spoken so Free!
But - Such Glee was to End!
For One Boy to His Will Refused to Bend!
He was a Lad
Who was Always Glad
NEVER to use Profane Language!
Which Meant He was a Real Sage!
The Contretemps Originated at the School Play -
Given in the Merry Month of May -
Many Hells and Damns Prevailed Throughout
That No One could do Without!
This Ogre Permitted
Not a Word to be Omitted!
This Boy Absolutely Refused
To Allow such Words by his Mouth be Used -
And All Month This Teen Raved -
For the Ogre He refused to Behave!
To the Ogre's Ears came This Horrid Blasphemy!
He called it a Terrible Catastrophe
As He Rumbled Forth from his Office Cave
To Make This Obstreperous Boy Behave -

Yet, He was not Exceptionally Kind -
The Pupil declined to Change His Mind
Which brought About a Nasty War
That On and On Wore -
Finally, The Ogre Commanded
That the Boy must be Reprimanded -
Said the Ogre, "For This Atrocious Evil
I Compare You to a Boll Weevil
Which Destroys the Cotton
As MY RULE You have Forgotten!
Now Leave these Grounds
That This School Surround
And DO NOT Return
Until You shall Learn
How to Cuss
In Order to Raise a Big Fuss!"
So, The Ogre his Anger Vented
Yet the Boy NEVER Relented!

CANTO III

A Grim Wife had the Ogre He
Who NEVER had Time to be Free -
This Wife - Porgy - Felt O so Low
While She Endured and Obeyed his Every Bellow -
The School She did not Run
Which Really wasn't much Fun -

My Life in Reflection

Other High School Heads
Had Their Feet Full of Lead
As Their Wives controlled Them!
So, You See, Why Ours was Exceedingly Prim -
This Porgy was Clearly so Unfair -
For not a Thing did she Care!
Now, Our Play I have told You About
So, at the Following Incident don't Pout!
Porgy had an Idea
That was not oh so too Clear -
She just Loved Clothes of any Type
Especially Tight-Fitting Blouses and Girl's Tights!
Plus, Dresses Showing the Contour of One's Lissome Hip
Made our Porgy just about Flip!
She would Rant and Rave
Because Sexy Skintight Dresses She Did Crave!
A Nice Photographer There Was
Who over Picture Taking made a Loud Buzz!
One Day He Desired for Advertising
Pictures of a Girl That were Truly Appetizing!
Of a Certain School Actress He took Shots -
And She wasn't Wearing any Polka Dots!
She Sported a Rather Sexy Apparel -
And She wasn't inside a Barrel!!!
Tight Tights of Blackest Black
That Looked like They contained Shellac -
She Displayed Her Brief Garb in Many Pictures
Which changed with various Seductive Mixtures -

In Each and Every one Appeared This Girl
Who Knew How to really Twirl!
Now Let Me Tell You Full and True -
How Porgy Turned Incredibly Blue
When She Viewed Erotic Pictures so Sexily Cute
She Wanted to Dash out and Play upon A Lute!
Of Course, the Public wouldn't Mind
To See a Brief-Clothed Girl of such a Kind -
Dressed in a Sexy and Provocative Mood -
For Play Practice definitely wasn't That Crude!
Immediately of the Pictures did Porgy Approve -
For She Feared No Public Reprove -
She Knew Tights the Public would Like!
So, Porgy Mounted her Bike
To Distribute the Pictures Taken
So, the Shocked World would be Shaken!!
But some Wives thought her Act
Was like a Stab in the Back!
Other High Schools did Their Husbands Head
And They, Too, Had Feet of Lead
So, When These Harridans Their Disapproval Vent
Porgy was Smoking a Cigarette Brand named Kent
In Horrible Outrage
Porgy turned into a Wizened Sage!
Quickly on the Smoke did She Strangle
And Turned True Blue at every Angle!
These Women's Condemnations She NEVER Forgave -
As She went right to Her Grave!!!

CANTO IV

From out of the Elramebla Hills
Where many a deer He Kills
The Ogre brought Hunting to his Assistant
A Man most Excellently Competent -
The Son of God would have to Admit
No Better Man for This Job was Fit!
All over the County This Man was Known
For the Sweetest Accent He was most Renown!
This Fellow was named The Ghoul
And He thought He was . . . O So Cool!
Many Teen Girls did He Bother -
Who Always Wished Him to Clobber -
Most of the Time He pestered Them at Lunch -
Preying upon Them while They Drank Punch -
He just Loved Them to Pinch -
And They, in Turn, Wished Him to Lynch!
On some Pretty Girl He Would Pounce
Whereupon away She would Flounce -
He would go Skipping Merrily Madly after Her
For Nothing would He Deter -
Intercom Announcements He Loved to Make -
About Student Cars Parked Wrongly - Or by Mistake!
The Teens would Love These Speeches to Hear
Because His Voice was so Elucidating and Clear!
There were some Girls Who Him Hated
And by Jokes Him They Baited -

Wearying of being Teased like This -
The Ghoul decided to End Each Student's Blessed Bliss -
Because Every Single Day -
They would make Him Pay -
The Ogre a Silly Law had Made -
Textbooks upon the Tables Must be Laid -
The Students Always set Their Books on the Linoleum Floor -
The Ghoul Announced in a Voice Ever so Clear,
"No More!"
He Forced Them to do This Again and Again -
Until Their Tempers to be High Began -
They would Their Textbooks Deliberately on the Floor
Leave
Such Disobedience the Ghoul couldn't Believe!
So . . . By Remarks Rather Crude -
He Made Disparaging Comments about the Cafeteria
Food -
The Students This Abhorred -
They Hated Him All the More!
But . . . One Day . . . On an Evil Plot
The Students Hatched and Threw in Their Lot!
They Held a Top-Secret Conference -
Only a Few were taken into Confidence -
After Calling His Bluff!
They Decided Him out to Stuff -
Into a Nasty, Smelly, Rotten Garbage Truck!
Hoping to have some Luck -
By Ridding Themselves of Him Forever -

Truly . . . Indeed! - They were most Clever!
For More Garbage to have Room
Each Load is Squeezed as Flat as The Moon!
His Stinking Fate was Sealed -
If No One Squealed!
On the Day of Doom They awaited His Approach -
Just like a Slimy Brownish Roach
That Evilly Awaits the Advent of his Prey
So He may have a bit of Food That Day -
At the Dropping of a Book The Ghoul was Attacked
And He in Defense Sadly Lacked -
His Screaming Voice could be Heard -
As He was Hoisted up and Carried Away by the Student
Herd -
They Dragged Him to the Truck of Garbage -
Which Contained Death, Refuse, and Rubbish!
They Tossed Him In
And Started the Slow Compression Bin!
Alas, Alack the Sweet-Voiced Ghoul Died -
Among the Food He had so foolishly criticized!

CANTO V

Porgy and The Ghoul had Lost
And Their Deaths Him Greatly Cost -
The Ogre Now knew it was his Turn
But had no Idea that he was to Burn!

To Butcher Him like A Cow
The Students Knew How!
Indeed, The Ogre's End was Near!
Although How, to Him, it was Not so Clear
There was, at This Time, The Ball in the Basket Tournament
To Which our Boys Went -
They Won a Game 39-36 the First Night
So They All decided the Next Day to Sleep Tight
And Slept In until Twelve -
The Ogre into Their Late Excuses did Delve -
Classes They had Missed due to the Game
Making the Ogre just a tad bit Insane!
He Declared Each Athlete a Hundred was to Receive
Because He had not given Them Leave -
Now This was an Extremely Foolish Move
Which was His Death to Prove -
For - a Hundred was Equal to Zero!
So All called Him the Second Nero!
The Students Rioted at This Fate
Because the Ball in the Basket Team had Slept Late -
"Take It Back!" They All in Anger Yelled -
But The Ogre would not be Impelled -
He Now Knew it was His End -
So to Their Will He refused to Bend -
Due to His Ridiculous Decree -
He was No More from This Life to be Free -
The Students decided to Burn Him at the Stake
For His Misguided and Horrible Mistake!

My Life in Reflection

Hundreds of Textbooks were Applied
Around the Flagpole Where He was Dragged and Tied -
The Fire was Quickly Lit -
And He was Gone Lickety-Split!
This Story, My Friends - I Swear! Is Perfectly True -
I would not NEVER Lie to You!
So - Please This Tale don't Rue!
'Tis the Custom for the High School Crew
If High School Heads are Unmindful and Cruel -
The Students - By Force . . . Shall Rule!
And the Ogre was not yet the First -
Among Those so Cursed
But Took His Place in Line -
And was the Third of His Kind -
The Triple-Headed Ogre Who was so Mean -
Not to Give Warning and Always Fight Clean.

This poem was an assignment for my senior year English Class at Albemarle (Elramebla, which is Albemarle spelled backwards) High School (AHS) in Charlottesville, VA, in 1964. The class was taught by Ben F. Turner (The Muse), an incredibly gifted teacher who sadly took his own life in the 1970s. Written in the style of *The Rape of the Lock* by Alexander Pope (1688-1744), it mocks the Principal (Ogre) and his wife (Porgy) who also taught at AHS, plus someone (The Ghoul) whose name I have forgotten but who may have been the Assistant Principal.

Chapter 4

M. A.

M. A. was a woman who had a profound influence on my love life and how I discovered both real and physical love for the first time, after I returned from Vietnam. We were introduced on September 4, 1971, by my best friend David, who sadly is no longer with us (RIP). I fell madly in love with her and hoped that we would marry. Alas, that was not to be. We dated over a year before she found someone else and broke up with me. The despair I felt at her loss was agonizingly unimaginable. Having lost her left me totally adrift and deeply angry at what I then perceived was a horrible betrayal. I poured out my loss in the poetry related to her as I was a tortured soul for several years after her departure. Now, over fifty years later, the pain of losing her still troubles my mind occasionally.

JOY TO MY WORLD!

Joy to the World!
Joy to My World!!
She has arrived and I am Happy!
I'm in Love!
I'm in Love!!
I'm in Love!!!
It's a Wonderful Feeling!
I have Searched - But She found Me!
I had Despaired - But, Unexpectedly -
She Appeared!
The Perfect Answer to a Long Quest -
How Could I Be so Incredibly Lucky?
My Prayers are Answered!
She has Appeared
To Free Me from Worry!
I Know I Love Her -
In so Short a Time!
But, I Dare Not Speak
For Fear of Destroying -
What I Hope to Be -
What I Pray to Be -
A Beautiful -
A Lasting - -
A Loving - - -
Relationship.

I Pray to God for Guidance -
I Pray to Him
Not to Blow My Cool -
I Pray to Him -
For Her to be the One -
I Pray That She Will - - - in Time
Love Me -

Joy to the World!
Joy to My World!!
For Once - Happiness!
Lord, You have been Kind!
You Led Me to Her -
She is so Cute -
So Sweet -
So Wonderful -
So Exquisitely Petite!
I have NEVER Experienced
So much Happiness!
Please . . . God - Make it Last -
Let Her come to Love Me -
I have often Wondered
And Doubted -
In Love – Love at First Sight!
Yet, Lord, What is This I Feel
Deep Inside Me?
It is the Happiness
And Pure Unfiltered Joy of Love!
How this could happen to Me

My Life in Reflection

Is Beyond Belief!
Yet, Fate does Mysteriously Move -
And it Brought Me to Her!

Joy to the World!
Joy to My World!!
Lord - Please Guide Me -
Give Me the Patience -
Give Me the Restraint -
Give Me the Will -
Give Me the Power -
Not to Ruin This!
All is Right Now -
Lord, I Pray to You -
Please Help Me -
Please Help Us -
Make a Life Together!
Thank You, Lord -
For M.A.

ODE TO M.A. #1

Loneliness is Such a Sad Affair -
And I can Hardly Wait -
To Set My Eyes upon You -
Again!
To be with You -
Again!
To Hold Your Lithe Body -
Again!
To Make Love with You -
Again!
You Took Me by Surprise -
I Didn't Realize -
I would Fall in Love with You
As soon as I Did!
Until I found Myself -
Helplessly Enmeshed in Love
And Sacred Adoration for You -
Yes, One is the Loneliest Number -
But Someone like You -
Makes it Hard
For Me Even to Think
I could Ever Live
With Anyone Else
Other Than You!
You Make it Easy

My Life in Reflection

For Me to Freely Give You My Heart -
NEVER Thinking 'Bout Myself -
My Eyes Cry Every Night for You -
My Arms Long to Hold You Again -
Because being with You -
Is Pure Unadulterated Nirvana!
Love is Beautiful Surrender
To Your Sweet Loving Lips -
To Your Lovely Warm Encompassing Arms -
How Wonderful My Life Now Is
Because You're in my World!
It's so Easy to be Proud of You -
Girl - I Love You!
Girl - I Love You!!
Girl - I Love You!!!
I Only Want to be Close to You -
No One Else -
So, NEVER Forget That You Told Me
You Loved Me -
And how do I so Love You!
And I'm sure We can make it Together
If Our Love Light
Burns On through Endless Time!
To Quote a Phrase -
In Erich Segal's Book, *Love Story* -
Love Means NOT EVER Having to Say You're Sorry![2]
But I'll always be telling You -

---

2 Erich Segal. *Love Story*. New York: Harper & Row, 1970.

I'm Sorry -
For Not being Good Enough -
To Deserve such a Wonderful Person -
Who will Always be in Love with You -
Give Me Your Hands -
Open Wide Your Arms -
And When You Kiss Me -
Remember -
I will Always Honor and Cherish
Only You - M.A.
Stay with Me M.A. -
Be a Part of the Rest of my Life -
Let me Show You How Many Ways -
I Will Always Love You!

ODE TO M.A. #2

I Gave You My Love -
And . . . For a Brief While, You Took It -
And You returned it with Yours -
But . . . Now All is Lost!
And . . . I Am Left Alone
Again . . . Again . . . Again
How Many Times
Has That happened to Me?
How Many more Times will it Happen?
We Loved and Made Love -
And We were One with Each Other -
But Then, Something Happened
And Our Relationship Disintegrated -
Before I Knew It - You were Gone!
Taking with You -
My Love .
My Heart . .
My Mind . . .
My Soul . . . .
God Surely knows How much I Loved You -
Only You!
There Could be No Other
Our Embraces were like Life Eternal -
Now You are Gone -
And Here I am Alone Again -

So many Things We Shared -
So many Things We Did - Together -
I Loved to lie in Bed with You and Talk
Your Smell Was . . .
So Clean!
So Fresh!!
So Exciting!!!
Your Scent is Still Here -
In my Bed -
NO!!! Our Bed!
But Now, You're Gone -
And Here I am Alone Again -

Waking up to Find You Staring at Me
Was such Joy -
You were so Precious -
You were so Cute -
Just like a Little Church mouse -
And Now, All I Have Left
Are some Badly Taken Pictures
To Remind Me of You -
There is Nothing Left Now -
But Memories for Me to Survive On -
Our Favorite Three Dog Night Song
Was "Joy to The World"
Now . . . There is No Joy -
Now . . . There is Only Sorrow -
Now . . . There is Excruciating Pain -
Now . . . There is Unfathomable Heartache -

My Life in Reflection

And Lastly . . . Horrible . . . Wretched
Unhappiness -
You Passed through My Life
Like a Ghost Ship in the Night -
Then Left Me Marooned -
And Here I am Alone Again -

How many Times will I Weep for You?
Until the Pain is Gone?
How much Time must Pass
Until You are Only a Vague Memory?
You Hurt Me Deeply -
You Kicked Me When I was Down -
I NEVER Thought You would do That!
I NEVER Thought You Were -
That kind of Woman -
But You found Someone Else -
Someone to Complement You at Every Turn -
And I Didn't?
I Offered You Marriage -
Yet, You Put Me Off -
I Gave You My Love -
But You Rejected It!
I Gave You My Life and You . . .
Ripped it Apart -
Disemboweling it - and ME!!
Until . . . All That was Left
Was Me - Now Broken, Torn, and Lost -
Crying Out for You to Return

Although You Grievously Hurt Me -
I Still Love You!
Still Want You!!
Still Desire You!!!
No One will Ever take Your Place -
So, I Sadly Mourn Your Departure -
Knowing -
I will **NEVER** See You Again!!!
You Are Dead!
Yet . . . Not Dead!
The Ache I Still Feel for You is Real -
I Try to Stop the Pain -
I Try to End the Mental Hurt -
I Try to Sleep at Night -
But I Can't!!!
God - How I Wish Time would Pass -
And Heal This Painful Wound!
I shall Carry it Always - And Remember You
With So Much Love Left in My Heart -
But, Here I am Alone Again -

Alone . . . Alone . . . Alone . . .
The Agony of Loneliness -
Is a Hell not to be Envisioned
For . . . No One will Ever take Your Place
How many Times We made Love
I Know Not -
Yet, I Know, I Shared My Essence with You
And You Lovingly Took It Inside of You -

My Life in Reflection

Why? Why? Why?
Did You Deceive Me?
Why did You Crucify Me?
I NEVER really Hurt You
As You have done to Me -
I Said some Things That Pierced You -
I had not Meant it to be So -
I Loved Your Body -
Your Sweet Tasting Breasts -
Small They Were -
But just Right for My Lips - -
My Mouth - - -
My Fingers - - - -
Did You not Realize
I Worshiped ALL of You?
You Taught Me the Smooth Curves -
And Sweet Tasting Crevices
Of Your O so Virginal Body
So That I came to Love -
Every Part of You -
Touching -
Feeling - -
Kissing - - -
Being Inside You - - - -
Something I NEVER had Experienced -
With any Other Woman
Now, Here I am Alone Again -

The Greatest Joy of My Life is Gone -
You . . . Were . . . That . . . Joy!
I Once Thanked Heaven for Meeting You -
Now, I Curse it for Separating Us -
FOREVER!!!
You Cried When You Read the First Poem
I Wrote for You -
I Wonder What You Will Do -
If You Ever Read This?
Will You Cry?
Will You Weep?
Or Will You Simply Laugh
And Smile Mischievously?
Then Say - Thank God! I Hurt Him
As He Hurt Me!
I Remember When I Said
"I Love You!" for the First Time -
And You Cried -
In a Previous Poem to You I Quoted
From Erich Segal's Book *Love Story* -
"Love Means NEVER Having to Say You're Sorry" [3]
But I'll Always be Telling You, "I'm Sorry!"
Do You Remember?
I Guess That Quote is more than True -
I'm Sorry for Loving You -
For Not being Good Enough -

---

3 Ibid.

My Life in Reflection

For Hurting You -
For Wasting a Year of Your Life -
But I'm Not Sorry for Trying
To Solve Our Problems -
When You Turned Your Back -
You Turned Your Face
To Hide the Fact
You were Inadequate
When it came to Trying -
Had You Loved Me More
You Might have sat Me Down and Talked -
Now, I Wonder, if You Ever Loved Me at All?
Or . . . Was it all just an Act?
Was I Your Guinea Pig Experiment?
Or was I just a Convenient Excuse?
Someone to Use and Then Discard?
How could You Be -
So Cruel?
So Ruthless?
It Astounds Me!
Yet, I Truly Loved You!!!
I Pray for the Day -
When You can look Back
At the Carnage You Have Created
And Feel Sorry for What You've Done to Me
I Pray against Hope -
That We shall meet Again
At some Future Time -

But Here I am Alone Again -

And You Are . . .
GONE! . . . FOREVER!
I'll Probably NEVER Know
What Became of You -
You will just Fade Away into Oblivion -
And I will Always Wonder
Where You Are?
What are You Doing?
And Who's Loving You?
So, this is One Final Futile Plea -
To You -
From Me -
To Please Keep in Touch -
For, It's Cold to be Left Out -
In the Dark -
All Alone.

ODE TO LONELINESS - MY CRY AGAINST THE DECEPTIVE SEX

Who am I?
Where am I Going?
Why am I Wandering?
Will I Ever See the Light?
Again?
Or is it My Fate to Wander Aimlessly
Like a Wraith in the Night
Trying to Find a Body to Inhabit?
My Journey in Life is One-Third Through
And Still, I Roam Alone -
Seeking -
Looking - -
Wondering - - -
Why am I Cursed to be so Alone
With No Woman by my Side?
A Black Shadow Surrounds Me -
And I Walk Unnoticed
Passing People Every Day -
It is as if I am a Ghost -
They Walk Right through Me
Going on Their Frivolous Way
As if I Didn't Exist -

But . . . I am Alive!
I Must make My Mark -
Or . . . Have I Already?
And has the Climax of my Life
Passed Me Swiftly By
Leaving Me to go Down?
Ah, Yes! I Fear it is So!
Spurned by my Fellows -
Kicked Aside by Every Woman -
I Arise to find Myself
In a Bullfighting Ring -
Facing El Toro!
He stands There Proud and Strong
Pawing at the Dirt and Swishing his Tail -
I Taste the Dust in My Mouth
Along with the Smell of His Blood -
It is a Dusty Smelling Blood -
An Old Wound Opened Now -
Like Prometheus
Suffering the Torments of the Vulture -
I Arise from the Dirt
To Stand and Receive the Final Blow -
But it doesn't Come -
NEVER Will -
For I am in Hell -
My Fate is to go through Life
Getting so Close to Finding a Woman
To Live My Life With -

And Then being Kicked
Down . . . Down . . .Down
Once More I am Stomped Upon -
Again and Again and Again -
Until Finally My Mind
Attains That Final Plateau -
OBLIVION!
I shall care No More
What becomes of Me -
Or What Happens to Me -
Women will become a Blur -
Things to Manipulate -
To Use . . . Then Discard -
As by Them I have been Discarded
So Many Times -
For I, Too, shall have My Revenge
Upon Those Women
Who have Walked over Me!
I Will Strike Back!
Be it Now Resolved -
That I will Show No Mercy
No Kindness
To the Opposite Sex -
I, Too, Will Use Them
As They have Me!!!
I will Toy and Tantalize Them -
As They have Me!
And Then - Like the Wolf in the Fold

Will I Strike down at Them -
Until I Tire -
I will make them Pay -
For what They have Done to Me!
And I Shall Have -
No Mercy!

LOVE

What is Love?
Why is There Love?
Why does it Hurt So?
It is Sometimes - So Damn Terrible -
Leaving a Hemlock Taste in My Mouth -
To Be Swallowed
And make me Unhappy Sad -
I Hate It!
I Despise It!!
It has Burned Me Once Too Often -
God Damn Love!
Damn Women and All Their Perfidy!
This is the Last Straw!
No More can I Endure -
The Deceitfulness of It - -
The Pain of It - - -
The Hurt of It - - - -
I am Grievously Wounded -
NEVER again will I Trust Any Woman!
For - All They bring me is Pain and Sorrow -
The Days I Wept for Her -
The Days I Cried for Her - -
The Days I Bled Inside for Her - - -
And She Spurned Me!
She Laughed at Me!

Kicked Me When I Was Down -
And Then, Quickly Took Another Lover!
I Hate Love!
And All Women Too!
Love Took Me from Her -
Led Me On -
So, I Committed Myself to Her -
And She Castrated Me!
Left Me All Alone!
She Walked Away - Scot-free!
The Mental Anguish I Still Feel -
Dulls and Numbs All My Senses -
The Memory of Her Lingers On -
I Am Unable to Chase Her Memory Away -
It is like a Harpoon Barb Digging Deeper
Into My Brain and Driving Me Crazy!
All This - and More! - Love has Done to Me!
I Vow NEVER to let it Happen Again -
No More Involvements!
No More Commitments to any Woman -
Damn the Female Sex!!!
Deceitful Traitors!!!
Taking Pleasure in Making Men (Me) Miserable!
No More Misery Now for Me!
I'll Hate and Transmit That Bitterness Back -
Striking Back -
Hurting Them -
Eviscerating Them!

It will give Me so Much Pleasure
To See Their Pain -
To See Their Sorrow - -
To See Their Sadness - - -
In Their Traitorous Eyes!
They caused it in Me!
Now it's My Turn for REVENGE!
I Hope it Hurts!
I Hope it Pains!
I Hope it Makes Them Miserable!
Love - You will not Toy with Me Again!
Instead, I'll Now Use You -
To Toy . . . To Play . . . To Hurt . . .
As You Have Hurt Me -
Only Then Will I Be -
FREE!!!

A CRY FOR LOST LOVE

Here I am All Alone -
Wandering Aimlessly -
Trying to Find Myself
And Someone to Share My Life -
But it Now Seems -
A Bit too Fantastic
That Someone would want Me -
I Cry and Cry Inside -
And Still the Pain Sits There -
I Still See Her -
Still Touch Her - -
Still Want Her - - -
But She is Gone . . . **FOREVER!**
And Deep Down in My Gut
I'm so Sick at Losing Her -
Endless Nights I Toss and Turn -
Wanting Her Back -
But Sadly Realizing it's OVER -
Knowing it will NEVER Reoccur -
And Each Day
I Die a Little More Inside -
Hopelessness is My Cross -
For I will NEVER Find
Another Woman to Take Her Place -
She and I Entwined

My Life in Reflection

In a Bliss so Beautiful -
So Now All My Days Are Dark!
No Longer can I Make Love with Her -
Except - Only in My Mind and Dreams -
That Will Not Do -
I Need Someone to Love -
To Love the Way We Did -
And I Now I Feel All Alone
Because I Fear I NEVER Will -
Find Another Woman - -
Who Will Love Me - - -
Make Love with Me - - - -
The Way She and I Made Love -
And it is This Fear
That Drives My Dark Cloud
Of Depression and Mourning
Even Deeper -
I Pray for Relief
To Find That Special Woman -
But I NEVER Shall -
Too Many Hurts Have Felled Me
And I Am Unable to Climb Up Again -
So, Now I Sit and Brood
And Watch My Life Pass By
While I Wallow in Self-Pity -
Remorse -
Regret - -
Despair - - -

And Past Memories - - - -
All of Which are No Good -
But That is All I Have Left!
I Wish I were
More Outgoing -
More Friendly - -
Less Paranoid - - -
But Sadly, For Me, I'm Not -
I've Abysmally Failed!
Loneliness is such Hell -
Without Her I Cannot Live -
She Gave Me Uninhibited Love -
In Every Conceivable Form -
I Took it and Spoiled Myself -
I Gave Her as MUCH as I Could
Of Myself -
Which wasn't Enough -
I Guess?
So, One Morning -
She Walked - No! Crept Out!
While I Was Sleeping -
Leaving Me in the Cold -
Without a Word of Goodbye -
Left Me with My -
Sorrow -
Sadness - -
Pain - - -
And Memories - - - -

My Life in Reflection

Memories to Remind Me -
That NEVER again Will -
This Type of Love Happen to Me -
NEVER Again will I Find -
A Woman like Her -
Who Will Love Me -
Make Love with Me -
As She (and We) Did -
And This One Thought -
Scares Me So -
Frightens Me -
For I Cannot Live a Life Without
Someone to Love -
Someone to Desire - -
Someone to Share - - -
Someone to Couple With - - - -
And So it Seems
I must Now -
Prepare to Die!
Rather Than Living -
In This Tormenting Hell -
That Hounds Me Constantly -
Day by Day - -
Hour by Hour - - -
Minute by Minute - - - -
Second by Second - - - - -
I Cannot take Much More!
I Do Fear I am Cracking -

Under the Strain of Desperation -
And Futility -
In My Now Worthless Life -
And That kind of Love
I Shared with Her -
Really is only a Fleeting Shadow -
Which I Will NEVER Grasp or Hold -
Again.

ANOTHER WEEKEND

Another Weekend
Alone Again
Yes - Alone!
Alone . . . Alone Again
I won't have to Wait
For the Trailways Bus
It Won't be Bringing . . .
Her
Nor will the Train
No More Cheerful Greetings
For -
She Won't be Here -
NEVER Again!!!
God! How it Hurts!
She . . . Won't . . . Be . . . Here
This Weekend -
To Share My Bed -
No One to Touch -
Sleeping Next Me -
No One to Wake up With -
And Kiss -
In the Morning
And Make Love With -
Another Weekend
Alone Again

No One to Share -
My Saturdays
Or Sundays With -
She's Gone!
GONE! GONE!! GONE!!!
NEVER to Return!
I Weep Inside
And I Am -
So Deeply Saddened -
My Broken Heart -
Will NEVER Heal -
Nor will it Mend
The Hurt
Extends too Deeply
Into My Mind
And Will Not Heal -
For, It Is
Just Another Weekend
Of Being Alone
Again.

NO HOPE #1

Time is Nothing -
I Cannot Live Alone -
There is No Beginning -
Only an End -
My Cries Go Unheeded -
And I am Abandoned
To Aimlessly Wander -
Alone!
Dying a Little Each Day -
Until I am Nothing -
I'm almost There -
Because There is No Hope -
Hope Died Last September*
So Did I!
I'm a Walking Skeleton -
Hollow and Open -
Nothing is Left -
Just a Shriveling Shell -
An Empty Husk -
Because I am Nothing -
I NEVER was Something!
How I Wish Death -
Would Claim Me -
Take Me Away -

---

* September 1971 is the month and year that M.A. left me.

Cure My Ills -
Leave Me Free -
For I Cannot Stand -
This Cage -
Called Life.

NO MORNING AFTER

For Me There is No Morning After -
Only Despair -
And the Knowledge of the Hopelessness
Of This Thing called Life
Each Day is an Agony to Endure -
And I feel Crucified
Upon a Cross of Thorns
Each Waking Hour
Is an Unending Hell
Unbearable and Excruciating
My Life without Her is Void -
When She was Here
She was My World
Now She is Gone -
And I am Consumed
By the Desire to Withdraw
From This Thing Called Life -
For I Cannot Suffer More -
The Cross is too Heavy to Carry
Each Day of Loneliness NEVER Ends -
It Just Blends into the Next Day -
And so the Pain is Drawn Out -
The Pointed Barbs Stick in My Mind
Ever Deeper than Before
Why Must I Suffer So

While Others Adjust and are So Happy?
Why Cannot the Memory of Her
Fade, Blur, and DIE!!!
Why do I still Cry
And Cry . . . And Cry . . . And Cry?
Living without Her is Not Life.
I shall NEVER Recover
So it is Written - - I Must **DIE!!!**
I Wish I could find That
Sweet Peace -
Perhaps, One Day - I Will -
Soon!!!

LONELY NIGHTS, LONELY DAYS

Lonely Nights -
O How Many More
Will There Be?
Will I Have to Endure?
Lonely Days Too -
How Many of Those
Will I Have -
To Suffer Through?
Being Alone -
Isn't Really Kind -
Yet Fate Seems To Say -
This Will Not Be My Day -
The Excruciating Pain
Of Lost Love -
Still Resides within Me
And Will NOT Leave -
I Try to Close It Out -
But . . . It Always . . .
Returns -
To Remind Me
Of Lonely Nights
And Lonely Days.

THE MAGIC IS GONE

Where has All the Magic Gone?
And Why did it Disappear?
Leaving us Standing Here
Looking at the Clouds?
Why is it That Something Good
Always comes to an End
Leaving Me All Alone Here?
I am a Lone Figure -
Swept by the Pouring Rain
Along Desolate Lands
As the Wind Smacks My Face
And Water Drips from My Hat
I am Buffeted by the Boreal Winds
Which Howl and Tear at Me
As I Cling Desperately -
To the Ship's Rail -
Before I am Swept Overboard
And Plunged into the Raging Sea -
I Am Tossed . . . Turned . . . Tumbled
By the Waves
And Spewed up on the Shore -
Alone . . . Again!
The Receding Waves
Slap at My Feet
To Prove that Once Again

My Life in Reflection

All the Magic is Gone
Yes, It is Gone from Me Now
There is No Magic
Since She left Me
For . . . When She Left -
The Magic Stopped - -
The Laughter Stopped - - -
The Love Stopped - - - -
And I Stopped - - - - -
Because . . .
The Magic was Gone
Gone! Gone!! Gone!!!
And I am Forever Left Alone -
It's been Almost Two Years Now
And My Life is Still Shattered!
You Try to Pick up the Pieces
But They NEVER Quite Fit Together -
Before the Glass Shattered
You Can Rebuild
But I Haven't -
The Magic is Gone
And I -
I Have Built
A Mighty Fortress around Me
So That No Pieces
Will Ever be Broken Again!
I Ache to Give -
But My Magic is Gone

So Here Am I Alone
Waiting for the Impossible -
Dreaming the Impossible -
For to Dream a Dream
Is to Sleep -
And, Thankfully, in Sleeping
One Escapes This Thing
Called Life -
And . . . By Escaping -
We Miss the Magic Show
So, Step Right Up Folks!
And Watch the Magic
But Be Careful NOT to Participate
For . . . If You Do
You, Too, May Vanish like the Rabbit!
And Then Your Music is Gone.

Chapter 5

LOSS & LOST LOVE

Another major theme of my poetry concerns loss and lost love that I have experienced during the past sixty years. All of us have experienced some kind of loss during our lives — whether it be personal — or knowledge of a loss affecting other people's lives. In my case, my inability to have long-lasting and successful relationships with women both outside and inside of marriage (thanks to Depression and PTSD!), has over time, led me to pour out my frustration at what I perceive are perfidious women, which has invariably, led to much heartache on my part. Yet, the responsibility for ninety-five percent of the loss and lost love, falls directly on my shoulders and not the women I rail against.

** Previously published in *The Other Side: Mist, Mirrors & Strange Tales*. Phoenix, AZ: Fiesta Publishing, 2022. Used with the author's permission.

DISPARATE THOUGHTS

We All Cry -
For What Might Have Been -
But NEVER Was!

Scorned by Fate -
Burned by Love -
NEVER to see Happiness

By the Still Waters of the Sea -
Shall I Weep Tears for Thee -
And Long to be Set Free

That Which We Would Escape -
We Do Embrace.

DECEPTION

She walks on Silken Slippers
Down Her Wedding Aisle -
Dressed in Virginal White -
She looks All Prim and Proper -
But, She's Really Full of Guile!
And When She Says, "I Do,"
It Will Not Be True -
For She is Deceptive
And will . . . Eventually -
Break the Man's Heart -
And His Life -
Along with His Hopes and Dreams
As She did Mine.

ABOARD THE "WILLIE B"

It was a Fine Night at Sea
Aboard the Yacht "Willie B"
Only Us Three -
You and Me
And, of course - the "Willie B"!
I Shall Always Remember Thee
Sitting in the Shade
Of That Old Oak Tree
That Fatal Moment - - We
Decided on a Voyage at Sea
Just You and Me -
Aboard the "Willie B"
Out of the Harbor at Castle Tree
Slipped We
Aboard the "Willie B"
The Wind Blew to the Lee
And on sailed You and Me
But We had Not Counted on the Sea
Which Meant to Take You from Me
And from Me - - My Heart's Key
O, How the Wind Blew Free
Just a Quiet Night's Sail -
I thought
Just You and Me
Aboard the "Willie B"

But Neptune came for Thee
And You were No Longer Free
Up! Up!! Up!!!
Rose That Horrible Sea
And Washed over You and Me
It Took You Far Away from Me
That Day Aboard the "Willie B"
I Swam after Thee
But was washed by the Sea
Back to the Shores of Castle Tree
Now went Your Heart and Love from Me
Taken by the Cold Cruel Deep Sea
And, now When I Sail to Sea -
I Remember You and Me
That Night aboard the "Willie B"
That Night God Stole You away from Me
Aboard the Good Ship "Willie B."

When attending a boy's prep school in Virginia during the early 1960s, I had a teacher whose name was W. B. R. I used his nickname, "Willie," to pen these lines.

THE SHIP

I saw a Ship A-Sailing
Upon the Mighty Blue Sea -
So High . . . So Low . . . So Deep
So Calm . . . So Terrible -
In Joyful Glee That Day
And I Watched the Waves
Lapping Peacefully
Against Her Bright Red Hull
Not a Man saw I on Her Masts -
Or Upon Her Bridge That Day -
Her Canvas was Full of Wind
Her Bow Plowed Ever Onward
Into the Wine Dark Sea
Where was Her Captain?
Where was Her Crew?
How could She sail Alone -
Unmanned upon the Sea?
She sails Ever so Fast
That No One can Stop Her
And She Passed Me By
So Quickly -
So Easily -
On Her Mysterious Way
I Stopped .
I Thought . .

I Realized . . .
She Would NEVER Pass Me by Again
So, I Turned -
I Cried -
I Felt Her Loss in my Heart
Knowing She Was -
Finally . . . Irretrievably . . . Irrevocably . . .
Lost for All Eternity to Me
She had Disappeared Forever
How could I Stand like Stone
And Watch Her Pass
Out of my Sight
So Swiftly on Her Way?
I Know Not How -
But I Did . . . Unwillingly - Let Her Go
Too Quick! Too Quick!! Too Quick!!!
I Shouted!
But All was too Late -
Someone Else in my Place
Would also have Allowed
It to Happen to Him
And He, Too, could not Stop
Her Speed upon the Seas
He, Too, would Cry
And Know His Efforts
Were All in Vain -
The Sun Set
And I saw Her Silhouette

My Life in Reflection

Against the Azure Blue Horizon
As, Like the Sun, It Seemed to Sink
Beneath the Ocean's Waves
Thus, It was Gone -
So Silently . . .
So Quickly . . .
That No One will Ever be Able
To Prevent Her Passing You By
Ever so Peacefully . . .
Oh! What a Sad Sad Event!!!
She was Wonderful!
I Think That we Should
Be Happy
At Her Leaving
Yet, my Friend -
We should Mourn
Her Vanishing -
But!
Do Not Regret the Pleasure
She Brought to You
While You Lived and Loved Her
Cherish Her while You Can
And NEVER Forget the Swiftness
Of Her Passage during Your Lifetime
Enjoy Her -
For She will NEVER Return Again
During Your Life's Days -
Know This - My Friend
And You Shall Profit All Your Life.

HOW MUCH MORE MUST I ENDURE?

How Much More Must I Endure?
When will it Ever Cease?
Will I have to End it All?
Or Will I Eventually find Happiness?
Why have I been so Cursed?

Why Do I Always Fail with Women?
What Is Wrong with Me?

I've been thrown Away -
Discarded . . . Snubbed . . . Ignored!!!
And Every Time
I Form an Attachment -
I'm Shot Down -
Old Girlfriends Marry -
Leaving Me for Marital Bliss -
Old Paramours get Engaged -
I'm Hurt and Deeply Wounded
My Heart Cries Out for Mercy!
But There Is None -
Each Time the Knife Wedged in my Mind
Is Driven a Little Deeper -
And Then Evilly Twisted a Little More

My Life in Reflection

Why Do I Always Fail with Women?
What Is Wrong with Me?

I'm Sad . . . and Disheartened -
Hurt after Hurt Descends upon Me -
Rejection after Rejection -
I Cannot Succeed
And Cannot Bear My Single Life -
Surely, some Happiness will Await Me
Beyond the Pall?
Death? . . . No Worries!
Death . . . The Dark Blanket
That takes Me Away
From This Life I Now Fear to Face -
My Trials and Tribulations
Are Too Heavy for Me, Lord
I Can No Longer Obey My Instinct
For Self-Preservation -
Why Must I Grievously Hurt?
Haven't I Suffered Enough?
Haven't I Done My Duty?
Wasn't I Absolved
By What I Accomplished in Vietnam?
I'm Tired of the Heartbreaks
And Now, Cannot Go Further
Oh, How I Hurt and Ache -

Why Do I Always Fail with Women?
What Is Wrong with Me?

Please . . . Please . . . Please . . . God -
Give Me some Happiness -
Give Me Some Hope -
But You Haven't!
You know I've Tried -
Now, I No Further can Go -
During My Lifetime You have led Me
Down a One-Way Street
To Unhappiness . . . Sadness . . . and Hurt -
I Cannot Return -
It's 25 Years too Late!
I Refuse to further Suffer!
I GIVE UP!!!
I Wish I were Dead!
No One Really Cares!!
No One Will Help Me!!!
And . . . I have Tried Hard
To Help Myself but - To No Avail!!!

Why Do I Always Fail with Women?
What Is Wrong with Me?

Black Amorphous Beings -
So Inky Dark and Enveloping -
Ooze Stealthily Into . . .
And Penetrate My Crazed Mind!
I am not Me Anymore -
No more Torment . . . or Worry -
My Life must Now be Forfeit -

My Life in Reflection

'Tis Better I Find My Grave
Then to Suffer -
The Unkind Blows -
The Snubs -
The Innuendos -
The Get Losts -
All This I Can No Longer Endure -

Why Do I Always Fail with Women?
What Is Wrong with Me?

I'm Unable to Form -
A Meaningful Relationship -
With Any Woman -

I'm Spurned!
I'm Deserted!!
I'm Forgotten!!!
No One Really Cares -
I just can't Pick Myself Up -
I'm Down on the Canvas for the Count -
For the FINAL Time!!
It's No Fucking Use -
With Each and Every Women
I'm an Absolute and Abysmal Failure!
I can No Longer stand living Alone -
Life's Gauntlet - - -
Its Trials and Tests
Are just too Overwhelming -
I Gave My All -

I Tried to Help Myself -
Why Me? . . . Why Me? . . . Why Me?
Lord?

Why Do I Always Fail with Women?
What Is Wrong with Me?

Am I just another Tantalus -
Forced to Stand in a Pool of Water -
Under a Fruit (Woman's) Tree
With Low Hanging Branches -
Forever Eluding my Grasp -
And before I can Drink
The Water/Woman Will ALWAYS Recede -
Before I can Imbibe Its/Her Sweet Taste?

Why Do I Always Fail with Women?
What Is Wrong with Me?

My Loneliness Is -
So Excruciatingly Unbearable -
I can stand it No More!
Why - Everyone has Someone . . .
Yet – I have NO ONE!
Why Must I be Sentenced
To a Single Life –
While Others are Together?
I'm So Lonely . . . Lonely . . . Lonely
I Need a Woman to Love . . . Worship -
A Woman Who Will Love Me Back!

So, Why Is My Search to No Avail?
Why Must I Be -
Single?
Lonely??
And Unhappy???
While Others Live Together
Or, are joined in Wedded Bliss
Together and Happy?

Why Do I Always Fail with Women?
What Is Wrong with Me?

It's NOT FAIR God!
And You Know It!
I'm No Christ for You God -
I . . . NEVER . . . Will . . . Be!
Yet - You Persecute Me!
You Torment My Mind!
To a Point Where -
I Even Doubt Myself!
The dull Edge of My Sanity
Wears Thin Lord -
And I am so Desperately Alone -
Yea - Tho' I Fear Thee Lord
I Hate Your Evil -
Which Besets Me like a Demon -
A Fiend!!!
From the Burning Fires of Hell!!!
I've Searched for the Elusive Solution -

But Still, There is No Fucking Answer -
At Least, I cannot find One in My Soul!
Even That, God, You have Taken
From Me -

Why Do I Always Fail with Women?
What Is Wrong with Me?

My Candle Now Burns Low -
The Rekindling Best be Soon -
Or - I Fear There may Be
But One Omnipotent Answer
And I shall Break Your Law -
You made Us Two for Two -
But Have Rebuffed and Denied Me!
I See a Hellfire Light Now Approaching
To Strike Me Mercilessly Down
And Sweep Away ALL My Ills -
Do You Think It Will?

NO MORE HURT, PAIN, SORROW, SADNESS

I Hate Love -
It Hurts Me Far Too Much!
I Cry Out for It -
I Begged for It - -
I Reached Out for It - - -
And it Encircled . . . Caressed -
Then Deceitfully Stabbed Me!!!
In the Back!!!
I Despise and Hate -
Its Perfidious Arms!
Love is a Traitor -
An EVIL EVIL EVIL Betrayer -
Why L. Did You -
Do This to Me?
Why did You Lead Me On?
I'm so Weary of Being Hurt -
And Ignominiously Rejected -
I am Led Down
A One-Way Street -
Of Hurt, Pain, Sorrow, Sadness

The Pain of Love
Is Nothing More
Than a Bitter Cup of Hemlock -

It Burns You -
All the Way Down!
It Tears Your Insides Apart!
And . . . Now . . . You are No One . . .
Searching for Someone -
Who comes Along
To Trick .
To Deceive . .
To Wound You . . .
With Hurt, Pain, Sorrow, Sadness

I want to Cry so Badly -
That it Hurts!
I want to Kill!
My Body Cries Out for Vengeance!!!
Yet, I Wish I Could Die!
But Then, I'm Too Cowardly -
I Cry, Instead, From -
The Hurt, Pain, Sorrow, Sadness
I Cry for Help
Yet Receive No Answer -
L.
Why . . . Did . . . You . . . Hurt Me?
Why was I Your Fool?

I really Played Your Puppet -
Didn't I?
You Used Me -
You were far Too Unkind -

My Life in Reflection

TOO TOO Cruel!!!
O God I Hate -
What Love has done to Me
I HATE LOVE!!!
I really let myself Go -
Overextended Myself -
To Hurt, Pain, Sorrow, Sadness

I reached out for Something
That I Knew would NEVER Happen -
Because, Love Avoids Me -
I Loved You - - L.
Like I NEVER Loved Before
And, yet You Deceived . . . Tricked Me!
You Led Me On -
And On -
To Hurt, Pain, Sorrow, Sadness
DAMN You To Hell!!!

This poem was written about a woman whom I dated shortly after returning from The War in 1970. A former high school girlfriend, L.B.G., (still a good friend after fifty-eight years!), introduced us at a party she threw for me to celebrate my return from Vietnam. The two women were roommates.

THOUGHTS

What Was
Can NEVER Be -
What Should Have Been
Will NEVER Pass - -
What Should Be
Will NEVER Be - -
Because Time
Cannot Be Relived
To Alter
What Cannot Be Altered
Is to Dream
The Impossible Dream - -
And To Dream - -
Is To Die
A Little Bit Every Day
Life Without Her
Will NEVER Be - -
Can NEVER Be Again
And So I Die
A Little
Each Day.

SEARCH FOR HAPPINESS

I Hate You Love!
I Hate What You've Done -
You've Hurt Me . . . Wounded Me -
I'll NEVER Allow You to Enter
Into my Life Again!
I Hate the Pain -
You Bring!
I Still feel it in My Gut -
I Hate the Sorrow
You Bring!!
For - I'm Unhappy Sad -
You've Torn Me Apart!
Ripped Me Wide Open!
Shattered My Hopes . . . My Dreams!!
Destroyed My Happiness -
You've Made Opened Thighs
An Entry Point for Abomination!
Loving Words and Gestures
Have become a Nefarious Cover
For Your Insidious Lies!
And There is No Trust -
Only Traitorous Betrayal!
And it's All My Fault -
For, I Tried to Love -
Tried to Care -
But I was Grievously Betrayed!

Thus, am I Nothing More Than -
A Total Failure?
A Loser in My Miserable Life?
I Vainly Search for Happiness -
Just a Small Thing -
Which Evades Me
Why can't I catch It?
Why Must I Suffer?
Aren't I Human?
Every Day I Cry -
More and More
And get No Nearer -
I Want Someone to Love -
Make Love To -
Be With -
Yet, I Futilely Chase the Elusive Butterfly
Of Love -
A Nondescript Dream -
For I Dream of Happiness
That NEVER Comes -
And I Wait for It

But No Woman Comes
To Share My Dreams
And Enjoy Life the Way
I Desire to Live It
Perhaps - One Day
It Will End . . .
My Search for Happiness.

UNHAPPY SAD #2

Pray Tell, My Friend -
What is it Like
To Be Unhappy Sad?
'Tis Wishing She was There -
Knowing She won't Be -
It is the Knowledge
That You are . . . Indeed . . . All Alone

Can You Tell?
Can You See?
I Am Unhappy Sad -

For I cannot Wash it Away -
It's an Indelible Stain -
And I Am Left
To Bear the Weight
Of a Hundred Mistakes -
And Verbal Faux Pas

Can You Tell?
Can You See?
I Am Unhappy Sad -

Each Time I Venture Forth
I Am Afflicted
With a Leper's Curse -
I Try to Surface - Frantically!

Yet Sink Deeper and Deeper
Into the Mire!
I Cry Out in Pain -
Yet Swallow More Hurt -
Why Am I So Cursed?

Can You Tell?
Can You See?
I Am Unhappy Sad -

My Search for **THE** Girl
Will NEVER End -
For - I shall not be Content
Until I have Captured -
That Beauty -
Nor will I Rest -
Until I find Her -
And . . . Until I Do
I will NEVER take Less
Than That for Which
I Search!

Can't You Tell?
Can't You See?
For - I Shall Forever Be -
Unhappy Sad.

IT'S A LONG WAY COMIN' DOWN

As I Walked Through Your Life
You Deeply Affected Mine
And I was Oh so Kind
I Begged for Your Pardon -
For my Sins and All -
But You Turned Your Back on Me
Yes - You Did!
You Turned Your Back on Me!

It's a Long Way Comin' Down
And I Thought I'd Die -
But - You Turned Your Back on Me -
And Shot Me Down!

When You Deceived Me So -
Why, Oh Why?
Did You Shoot Me Down?
Why was I Your Puppet Fool?
I Loved You in Every Way
But - You Shot Me Down -
Yes - You Did!
You Shot Me Down -
You went Your Own Way -
And Ignored My Love -

It's a Long Way Comin' Down
And I Thought I'd Die -
But - You Turned Your Back on Me -
And Shot Me Down!

I Tried to be a Part -
Of Your Life -
But You Shut Me Out -
Closed the Door!
Yes - You Did!
You were too Deceptive
And Won Your Little Game -
So, I Threw My Towel In

It's a Long Way Comin' Down
And I Thought I'd Die -
But - You Turned Your Back on Me -
And Shot Me Down!

You Watched Me Comin' Down -
You Planned it All -
Oh Yes - You Did!
You Watched Me Fall -
And Hurt Me Oh So Bad!
I Tried to Fly for You -
But - You Shot Me Down
You Shot Me Down -
I Fell to the Ground -
And Watched the Clouds Move Past

My Life in Reflection

It's a Long Way Comin' Down
And I Thought I'd Die -
But - You Turned Your Back on Me -
And Shot Me Down!

And Now - I'm ALL Alone -
Without Your Smiling Face -
Without Your Sparkling Eyes -
With a Mischievous Twinkle in Them -
And . . . Without Your Warm Lips -
For Me to Kiss and Love You
Still —

It's a Long Way Comin' Down -
And I Thought I'd Die -
But - You Turned Your Back on Me -
And Shot Me Down!

This was written about L., who was mentioned in an earlier poem.

BEING ALONE ISN'T KIND

Being Alone isn't Kind -
Actually - It's a kind of Crime -
Alone . . . Unattached -
Wandering in Search
Of Something Lost and Gone -
He often Wonders Why
He Trudges Alone
Without a Wife -
Without a Female Companion -
So, On He Walks -
Searching for That Special Woman
Aching . . . Crying Out!
Hoping against Hope to Find Her -
Yet Hurting Ever so Deeply Inside
Because His Search is in Vain -
He Sees a Woman -
In a Store -
On the Street -
At the Country Club -
Anywhere!
But He can't Meet Her
He's too Timid - - - or Afraid to Speak!
And so He Dies a Little More
Within Himself -
He Sees Others Dating -

My Life in Reflection

Pairing -
Kissing - -
Mating - - -
Yet, He Watches All Alone -
Who Best Knows His Pain
But Only He Himself?
Floundering - - - He Struggles -
To Save Himself -
Only to Sink Deeper
Into the Quicksand -
Of a Lonely Life -
Oh! Wait!!
There's a Pretty Woman!
Alas Damn It!
She's Taken -
Forget Her!
That Woman across the Room -
Why Not Approach Her?
Damn! Her Date Stands Nearby!
Forget Her!
We are All Trapped within Ourselves -
In a Tremendous Struggle
Of Self-Restraint -
Unsure . . . Unwilling -
To Take That First Step -
He Lives with the Pain
Of Knowing Everyone Else
Is Happy

And He Isn't!!!
No One is Left
From the Old Crowd
Who isn't Paired
Or Physically Joined Together
In Passionate Love -
The Sadness of it All -
Is That No One Else
Realizes His Excruciating Pain -
They're All Too Wrapped Up -
In Themselves -
So, He Stands Outside
Looking In -
Searching for a Lifetime Mate -
His Ideal -
Beauty and Slimness -
He Desires -
After All -
Everyone Else Does!
And They Find It!
Why Can't He?
Pondering This Question -
He Wonders What's Wrong -
And Slowly Begins to Realize
That He Awakened Too Late -
It's really Not His Fault Tho' -
He Was Shaped . . . Molded -
By Previous Untreated Trauma

My Life in Reflection

Of Childhood and War
And Now Has
Broken the Mold Far Too Late -
Too Late to Find Her -
Too Late to Have the Fun -
He Should Have Had -
Yes . . . It's Too Late
To Make Up for It!
All He can do is Hope
Because Being Alone Isn't Kind.

THE LEAVES

The Leaves Fell Today
All over the Streets -
And Sidewalks
Swishing and Swirling
Around and Around
Swaying Back and Forth -
Cradling Me as I
Wade Through Them
They Hold -
Grasp - -
And Caress - - -
Like a Beautiful Lover
Whose Arms Encircle -
Entwine - -
And Titillate - - -
Then Suddenly Disappear -
Blown Away by a Windy Gust
Falling Hopelessly by the Wayside
Like a Lover Who
Drops Her Warm Comforting Arms
Leaving You Out -
In the Mind-Numbing Cold
To Watch the Leaves
Swishing and Swirling -
Rising and Falling -

My Life in Reflection

Time after Time -
Until They are Dead and Gone -
Like the Silent Lover
Who Tiptoes Away -
And Silently Flees
NEVER to Return!!!

THE LIGHT IS OVER

When September Leaves
Begin to Turn
And October's Windy Blasts
Bear Down upon the Land
Where will You and I Be?
On Separate Lands?
On Singular Islands?
In the same Sea?
Miles Apart -
Yet within Reach
But Not within Touch
The Summer has Ended
And it is Time to Part
Our Beautiful Loving Idyll
Is Over
Leaving Us Incomplete
For Now We Diverge
And Go Our Opposite Ways
Our Summer Dalliance is Over
We were too much Alike
And couldn't Perceive
The Naked Truth -
You were Good -
And I was Evil -
And We Played our Parts Well
Yet, Neither Triumphed

My Life in Reflection

Over the Other!
And so, Our Chess-Like Stalemate
Developed Well
You Made Your Moves
And I Made Mine
And Neither One of Us
Really knew What was Happening
We were like Two Field Marshals
Jockeying for Battle Position -
Not really Achieving Much -
So, Our Impasse
Left Us Unsettled
You Left Me for Knowledge -
(And Perhaps Escape)
While I Remain Alone -
Bitter . . . Disappointed
Yet Not Unhappy
For I cannot Change
That Which is within Me
So, My Heinous Poison Persists
Within me as I Search
For Another Woman -
To Find -
To Taste - -
To Ruthlessly Devour - - -
I Wonder Who
Will be the Next One
To Repudiate Me?

THE LONELINESS AND THE HEARTBREAK

In the Night
When the Blackness Comes
And I Am All Alone
Then, Too, the Loneliness
And Heartache
Attack Me
Filling Me with Sadness
And Despair
Alone! Alone!! Alone!!!
No Warm Body -
To Lie Next To
No Mouth to Kiss -
Or Receive a Kiss From
No Loving Arms -
To Hold and Caress
No Pinkish and Erect Nipple -
To Suck On -
And Become Aroused
No Receptacle in Which -
To Deposit My Seed
For Love has Truly Vanished
And Seems Likely
NEVER to Return
Growing Old Alone -

My Life in Reflection

Waiting for Someone -
Knowing They Will
NEVER Again Appear
I Want to Love -
And be Loved
But Love . . . For Me -
Is Somewhat Elusive
Elusive???
Hell . . . It is Non-Existent!!
You Fool!!!
I Have No One to Blame
But Myself!
Yet I Wonder -
Yet I Ponder - -
And I Grieve - - -
That Others can be So Happy
While I Walk
Down That Long Narrow
Lonely Path
With No Woman by My Side
What a Price -
I have Paid!!!
How Much More will it Cost?
Will it Cost -
My Mind?
My Body??
My Soul???
I Think So!

I Believe That is the Price -
I must Pay
Life is One Continuing
Sadness after Another -
And I Must Trudge Through It
One Long, Long Day at a Time -
Always Wondering -
Will I Ever Find Happiness
In a Woman's Arms?
No . . . I Don't Think So -
After All -
I'm Doomed to Walk
This Path Called Life
Alone -
Forever!!!

TO KATHERINE

Love Is So Fucking Ephemeral -
It Rushes in like a Warm Summer Wind -
And Leaves You like an Icy Winter Blast
While You Have It -
You're on an Incredible High -
But . . . As in Times Past -
You know it will Leave -
After All -
You Were Born Not to be Loved -
So Love Mocks and Teases You -
Gently Caresses You
With False Hopes and Desires -
Then Abruptly Leaves You -
Standing out in the Freezing Rain
Shivering for a Brief While -
Until You Find It Again
Come On!
Let's Try One More Time!
Let's Go And Warm Ourselves
At the Fire Again
After All . . . It's Only Love!!!
It's Gonna Leave You -
Again . . . And Again . . . And Again
Many Many Times More -
You were Born to Wander

Through This Wretched Life
Alone! Alone!! Alone!!!
Each Time It BURNS You -
You Withdraw a Little More
Until You FINALLY Realize
It's just Not for You -
NEVER was for You!!!
Come, Let us Go Inside Now
And sit a While
No - - I don't think So!
It's Time To Give Up - - -
HOPE
It's Finally Time -
To Adjust to Solitude . . .
Forever -
It's Time to Die.

This poem was written in 1973 for a woman named Katherine, whom I had met. Now, I have no recollection of how I met her or how long I knew her.

AUTUMN

Falling Leaves
Drift Slowly Downward
Spiraling Their Lazy Way
To the Earth's
Rust Colored Floor -
They Stir and Quietly Rustle -
Lifting Off of the Forest Floor
Spinning -
As if in a Tiny Whirlpool -
Before the North Wind
Blows Them Along the Ground

It is the Autumn of My Years
As I Trudge Lonely and Cold
Through This Desiccated Landscape
My Head is Down -
Because I Still Look –
For The NVA Tripwires -
Knowing Full Well -
There will be None -
But Still Thinking about the Time
In the Jungle -
When There Were - -
I Was Young Then
Just One Score and Four!

Now . . . I am in My Autumn -
But . . . the Enemy's Tripwires -
Are More Ephemeral
Yet Life is Still Filled With -
Treachery and Deception
Especially Duplicitous
And Conniving Women
Who Insinuate Themselves
Into Your Life
And Then Leave You -
Grasping -
Tearing - -
Ripping - - -
Your Heart to Shreds -
Sucking it Dry -
Impaling It -
Upon Their Misbegotten
And Treacherous Souls
Then Twirling it Around
Sneering -
Laughing - -
Mocking - - -
Inwardly Despising You
So . . . I Walk Alone and Pensive

In My Autumn Years
I am Now Afraid -
To Commit Myself -
Or My Heart -

It's Easier just to Meet Them
Touch Them -
Kiss Them - -
Arouse Them - - -
Make Love to Them - - - -
Then Leave
Before They Grasp You
With Their Insidious -
Boa Constrictor-Like Talons!
Sticking Needles into Your Mind -
Tearing it Apart -
Like Sinuous Pythons -
They are so Unscrupulous!

Forget Love!
It's Really NEVER WORTH It!
Just Too Fleeting -
It's Better
To Enjoy a Woman -
In the Physical -
Than it Is -
In the Emotional
For . . . If You Commit Your Heart -
To the Unfaithful Bitch
Like a Raving Hyena
Or an Inky Colored Black Widow Spider
She will not Hesitate -
To Devour You Alive - -
Then Spit You Out - - -

And Move On - - - -
To Her Next Victim - - - - -
So Proud in Her Grace - - - - - -

So, Here I am in My Autumn -
Better . . . I Think . . . To Wander
Through the Woods
Scattering the Leaves -
Crunching Them Underfoot -
Putting the Past behind You -
And Moving Silently On -
Awaiting the Spring
And Another Fresh Bloom
To Pluck -
To Use - -
To Discard - - -
By the Time -
When Autumn Next Arrives.

Chapter 6

MIND DREAMS

The reader may think that I was under the spell of some mind-enhancing hallucinogenic drug while writing the following ten poems. I never ventured into that psychedelic realm! This section explores that dark side, which I believe is embedded deep within many of us. It is a side we dare not think about, much less discuss with anyone, but in fact, and maybe in truth, we secretly wonder what is really contained in the nether regions of our minds, our souls, or our psyche. We all have demons, whether we acknowledge them or not. Still, they are there waiting for the time when they may be called forth. I think a few of them may have escaped from me while I was writing the following section of poetry.

THOUGHTS RANDOM COME AND GO

All These Thoughts Coming and Going -
Who Knows -
When Will the Wind Stop Blowing?
But the Sea Will Rise Up -
To Splash Down upon the Sand -
Then Ebbing Back -
Into the Murky Green Depths
While Gulls Fly to Utah -
To See the Mormons
Now, Dust Blows upon the Red Sand
Of the Kalahari
Whose Kenyan Antelope Blissfully Graze
Unaware of the Deadly Tawny Lion
Lurking Nearby -
The Aborigines of Australia Grow Restless -
Where the Sea Laps upon the Distant Shore
And the Yellow-Red Sun Dies in the Western Hills
Where the Cowboy Ties His Horse's Reins
And Then Calmly Settles back for a Siesta Nap -
Leaving You and I Alone
To Watch the Moon Rise over Russia -
The Nazi Flag is Trampled
Underfoot into the Blood-Splattered Dirt
While Germany Rises -

More Powerful Than Ever Before!
The Dark Continent Finds Light
And Rises Up to Meet the Challenge -
While Men Riot in Buenos Aires
Against the Tyrannical Peron Regime -
The Fish Swim Peacefully in the Grand Banks -
Off Newfoundland -
As Europeans Fish in the North Sea -
Iceland Melts Away -
Into Greenland
And You Soar Over
The Atlantic Ocean in your Private
Ten-Million-Dollar Jet Plane
Touching down in Tehran -
To Be Warmly Greeted by the Shah
Who Kindly Asks You to Bide Awhile
While LBJ Shakes Hands In New York
RFK is Fighting for Votes -
The Vietnam War gets Exponentially Bigger -
Yet, Each War Year Rolls Endlessly On and On
Killing More Men while China Rumbles
To Spew Forth a Billion Men -
Japan Advocates Birth Control -
While the U.S. Accepts Abortion
The Spears and Arrows of the Papuan Natives
Sink into the Backs
Of Black-Frocked Catholic Missionaries -
Who Try to Teach That Christ is Good -

But - We All Know -
THAT GOD IS DEAD!!!
A Green Monster Rises -
From Out of Hell's Bowels
To the Sound of Resounding Bullets
Indiscriminately Fired by Charles Whitman
Bouncing Off the Texas Tower -
Female Butchers Become Doctors in Chad
Because the Custom of Female Genital Mutilation
Is Still Alive and Acceptable
In the Primitive and Ignorant, Tradition-Bound,
Unenlightened Black African Tribes -
On the Dark African Continent
While the Peace Corps starts a War
In Outer Mongolia
Bob Hope Still Visits Cape Horn -
To Entertain the Apartheidists!
A Half-Ton Botswanan Water Buffalo
Emerges Alongside the Shore -
Of the Okavango Delta -
Charges the Great White Hunter -
As His Bearers Yell -
A Frantic Warning of "Bwana!"
Too Late!
The Massively Dangerously Sharp-Hoofed Beast
Tramples, Gores, and Crushes Him Underfoot -
The Panama Canal Runs Dry
To Ensure That Monaco Conquers Europe -

Which - in the Long Run - All Goes to Prove -
We Are All So Fucking Crazy!!!
Humanoids Watch a Girl and Boy
Go Hand in Hand -
Across the Undulating Dunes of Eternal Time -
Sleep Comes and Whisks Us Away -
To Peter Pan's NEVER-NEVER Land -
That Land of Timeless, Endless, Childhood Dreams
Which Float Us Up and Away
Into the Mushroom-Shaped Clouds
Rising from China's Newest A-Bomb -
We Throw Our Scraps Away
For the Garbage Man to Eat
As He Watches the Martians Land
To Pulverize Us
With Their Solar-Powered Ray Guns
Which Then Melt like Chocolate in the Moonlight -
So That Caesar Can Return -
From His Moldy, Assassinated Grave -
To Save Us!
Wheels Go Spinning . . . Spinning
Faster and Faster!
Into an Indistinct Gray Blur -
Our Minds become Blotted and Besotted -
Due to the Ravages of Time Unending
Which Floats by Endlessly
Bringing Us to the Realization -
That Life is All Too Short

And We Waste It by Sleeping
We Should Love Life's Intricacies -
So - Open the Flood Gates
And Allow the Water to Carry You
Down Lethe -
Into Life -
Oh! All These thoughts -
Coming and Going -
Who Knows When the Wind
Will Stop Blowing?

ON THE THRESHOLD OF A DREAM

My Mind Is Spinning Me
Around and Around
Rolling Me Over and Over
The Waters of Time Wash Me
Cover Me, Soothe Me, Calm Me
I See the Strobe-Like Lights
Striking! Flashing!! Blinding!!!
The Dark Clouds Move Silently
Sweeping All before Me
They Are Destruction!
Vastness Awaits the Lone Survivor
Who Rises from the Rubble
A Skeleton with Rotting Flesh
Hanging Loosely on its Bones
The Broken Trees Lie
As If They Were Matchsticks
While the Brilliant Blinding Sun
Unmercifully Beats Down upon Me
I Am Parched -
Now the Rhinoceros Approaches
Swishing its Tail at the Myriads
Of Blood-Bloated Flies
Sitting on its Back!
The Silken Web of the Giant Tarantula

My Life in Reflection

Sparkles in the Sun's Cold Rays
Eight Bristling Feet - Fuzzy
Advance Upon Me
Its Sharp Beak Ominously Sounding -
Click! Click!! Click!!!
Like the Alarm Clock -
Awakening Me
I Climb from My Bed
And Step into the Past-Future
I Am Awed by the Immense
Smallness of Myself
The Dark Red Canyon Walls
Tower above Me
They Lean Down
To Whisper in My Ear -
Time! Time!! Time!!!
I Float - Then Drift
And Pick Myself Up
On a Beach of White Sand -
The Yellow Eyes Stare at Me
Blinking Again and Again
Probing the Inner Me
I Scream - But No Sound Comes!
Colors - - Red, Blue, Yellow, Orange
Bend, Fold, and Weave
Back and Forth
While the Snail Crawls Slowly By
Its Three-Foot Long

Antennae Reaching Out
To the Stars
Whose Powerful Lights Blind -
Then Recede
Like a Beating Heart
Radiating Out Into
The Pitch-Black Inky Night
While the Lion Peacefully Gazes
Over His Unchallenged Realm
And the Kalahari Winds Gently Blow
Wafting Over Him
My Head Feels like Exploding -
White Clouds in a Stark Azure Sky
Soft Green Grass Sways and Enfolds Me
Lying upon My Back
On the Rocky Hillside
The Vultures Circle Overhead
Crying! Diving!! Screaming!!!
A Dream to Remember.

THE TRIP

I Saw a Duck-Billed Woodpecker
Sitting on a Long -
Finger-Like Tree Limb -
The Limb was Thick -
The Tree was Small -
And Some Massively Huge Hand
Reached Out and Grabbed Me
In a Vise!
It was Gnarled and Veined -
Blue-Green and Wrinkled!
I Squeezed Out -
And became a Tiny Elf
Running through the Apple Orchard
Twisting . . . Turning . . . Stumbling
To Find Myself in a Labyrinthine Maze
Protected by Tall Hedges to the Sky
Yet, Now I Am Trapped
By the Evil Red Serpent -
With a Trident Flickering Tongue -
Slimy and Slippery -
Like a Body's Intestines
Slithering over My Feet -
Like a Thousand Slimy Thrashing Snakes
From All Over the Earth
So I Jumped Up to Find

I was Flying with Pterodactyl Wings!
I Soared High into the Heavens
Over a Stash of Untouchable Gold Bullion
Left by some Forgotten Buccaneer
Who Sailed upon the Steppes
Like Something Wicked Wonderful
Winding a HUGE Clock
That Ticks Off All the Seconds
We Have Left in Life -
Before We Float
Upon the Endless Sea.

Having NEVER tripped on LSD, this poem reads as if I have tried it and written about the experience.

WHIRLWIND

I Saw a Mighty Whirlwind -
Radiating Fire and Unbearable Heat
Projecting a Reddish Trident
With Blood Dripping from its Prongs
As the Devil's Evil Red Head Appeared
Smiling . . . Leering . . . and Staring
While He Emerges from a Hurricane
As if to Say, -
"I Told You So!"
The Cyclone Whirls in One Place
Standing Still -
Yet, Inexplicably Undulating.
Out of its Mist Emerge
Two Horrible Piercing Yellow Eyes
Of a Black Widow Spider
Which Keeps Staring Silently
At its Paralyzed Victim
Who Trembles -
Yet - Moves Not
Because the Widow's Prey
Has Now Become -
A Trussed Victim
Lying upon a Mayan Sacrificial Altar
And Is Being Offered Up
To an Unknown and Uncaring God

Who Requires His Sacrifice's Blood.
So Now the High Priest
Raises and Rapidly Plunges
His Black Obsidian Knife
Deep into the Man's Chest -
Rips Out His Heart -
(While His Sacrifice Is Still Alive!)
And Then Eats It –
Before the Victim's Dying Eyes!
Next the Feather-Clad Shaman
Greedily Drinks -
The Dying Man's Blood -
Which Drips Down His Face -
Until He Pauses
And Turns to Offer Me
The Remains of the Blood-Filled Cup -
But I Shake My Head
And Stand Firm
As I Watch Him Scowl -
Turn . . . And Drink Again
The Whirlwind Suddenly Appears
And the Priest Vanishes
Into a Molten Pillar of Fire
Shining So Intensely Bright -
That I cannot Stand to Look
Fast He Melted Away -
And I Am Left Alone
Upon That High Blood-Stained Altar

My Life in Reflection

Looking Down upon the Barren Plains -
Of the Parched Waterless Sahara
The Clouds Sweep All before Me
And . . . I Float in the Light
Rising Upwards
Wafting in Space
To View the Earth
Now Darkness Falls -
And Draws an Ebony Black Curtain
Across the Land
The Play Is Now Over
Now Tied and Tightly Bound -
I Am Thrown . . .
Into the Cenote -
I Am Sacrificed.

MY EYES

Here . . . Yes, Here
I am!
Pierce My Inner Depths
If You Dare!
But You Won't -
For My Penetrating Eyes Strike You -
Satanically Burning into You
Like an Indelible Cattle Brand
Tearing Deeply Inside Your Flesh -
Like Some Macabre Demon
And Cutting Out Your Very Soul -
Open - I Command You!
Reveal Your Innermost Secrets
To the Blood-Scarred World!
See the Silent Evil within Me
Watching You . . . Staring at You!
Try to Turn Away - - - If You Dare!
But My Eyes -
Will Chill Your Thoughts -
Will Search You Out -
Will Discover You -
Will Make You Falter -
Will Make You Turn Away -
Will Seize You!
Wrench Open Your Mind!

My Life in Reflection

And Watch Until . . .
You Beg for Mercy!
Scream for It!
While My Green Eyes
Deny You That Peace -
That Nirvana -
And Reach Out to Stab You!!!
They Will Hurt You -
Make You Cry!
Make You Beg for Bloody Mercy!!
All Because You Dared
To Hurt These Eyes -
That Sparkling - -
Worshiped You - - -
And Are Now Closed
To Glory -
To Worship - -
To Love - - -
Replaced by Hate
And Revenge!!!
They Bore into You -
Piercing Your Deceitful Soul - -
Seep into Your Mind - - -
Flow into Your Heart - - - -
And Take Satanic Pleasure
In Excruciatingly Hurting You!
Just as Much as You Hurt Me!
I Look at You -

Yet, See You Not!
For, My Eyes See More
Than Your Corporal Body -
They Penetrate Right Through -
To Your Wickedly Evil Soul!
You can't Meet Their Gaze -
For, I Have Reached In
And Grabbed Your Soul!
Jerked It Forth -
Throbbing!
Pulsating!!
Quivering!!!
I Draw It Out for All to See -
And Raise It High in My Bloody Fist
But Already
It Droops -
It Fades - -
It Dies - - -
Yes . . . DIES!!!
Your Blood and Courage
Is No More!
Deep within Me
Evil Rises Up
And Spreads Itself
To Cover Your Wicked Soul!!!
The Evil That Lurks within My Eyes
Follows You . . .
Blood from Your Soul

Now Drips from Them
To Revenge Me!!!
For What You Did -
To My Eyes -
Which Sparkle No More
At the Sight of You!

WANDERING IN A DREAM

Wandering through the Various Stages
Of My Mind -
I Chanced upon a Reptilian Monster
With Pointed Ears -
Twitching They Were -
His Eyes so Albino White -
A Thousand Hairy Arms had He -
With Squat Bow-Legged
And Spindly Lower Limbs -
He Twined and Wiggled
As his Brown Fur
Bristled and Smoothed Itself -
I Found My Fingers Were -
Dripping Wet with his Blood
Red! Red!! Red!!!
It was as it Dripped
From My Crab-Like Fingers
Into a Boiling Churning Pot -
Of Sickening Yellow Goo
With a Hundred Eyes Popping Up
And Staring at Me -
I Took a Wooden Cudgel
And Stirred the Cauldron
Into an Unfathomable Vortex
Around . . . And Around . . . And Around . . .

My Life in Reflection

Like a Rainbow's Arching Spiral -
Enticing Me down the Walls
Of a Cylindrical Tunnel -
I Float -
I Flow - -
I Walk - - -
Down . . . And Down . . . And Down . . .
Into an Evil Spider's
Malevolent Clicking Beak
Which Engulfs Me into the Void -
I Find Myself in a Black Heaven
Of Silver Shining Stars
As I Am Uplifted to the Throne
Of the Red Devil
Who Sits Grinning and Laughing at Me
After All He Says,
"Life's Nothing More than a Joke, Isn't It?"
The Red Devil's Laughter -
Echoes Off a Ceiling of Red-Hot Embers
With Ham-Shaped Fists -
He Bangs the Arms of His Fiery Throne
Which Now Turns Into -
An Elephant's Trunk!
Leading Me Down
Into a Cool Green African Glade
Amid the Blowing Wheat Lands of Kansas
Where I Am Left Standing
As My World

Swirls . . . And Swirls . . .
Spins . . . And Spins . . .
More . . . And More . . .
All Around Me
Pushing Me Down into the Soft Mud
And Unconsciousness -
Again!
I Sleep Well -
Don't You?
After All I NEVER Did Understand -
Why My Life Was Like This?

SPIRIT PRAYER CHANT

Oh
Lighter Than Light
Darker Than Dark
Come from the Darkness
And Let Us See Thy Face
Speak to Us,
And Let Us Know
The Secrets We Shouldn't.
Take Us by Our Hand
And Lead Us
Through Streets of Darkness
To View Those Souls
From the Departed Past.
Let Them Speak to Us
And Tell Us of What
Is to Come.
Open Our Blind Orbs -
To the Future
And Enable Us -
To Understand
Remove These Chains
From Our Eyes
So That We Can See
For This We Pray
Oh, Great Dark Spirit!

SATAN'S CHANT

I Am Satan -
My Evil Ways Await You
Command Me!
And the Spirits Will Awaken -
Will Arise
They are Yours to Seek -
To Find the Answers
That Only You Search For -
And the Winds of Fury
Will Whirl You on Your Way -
So Let Your Blood Chill -
As Dark Death
In a Wraith-Like Cloak
Beckons You Onward
With Her Bony Skeleton Hand
To Join Her Along
With the Grim Reaper!
Rise with the Spirits -
Drink Deep the Dark Blood
Of 100,000 Lost Souls
And Gain the Forgotten . . .
Knowledge
Of the Hidden Recesses
It Is Yours to Pick -
See!!

My Life in Reflection

It Awaits You!
Come My Beloved -
And Join with Me
In the Devil's Feast
To Lose Yourself
In the Writhing Arms
Of My Dark Beings
For When the Midnight Hour
Strikes Its Doomsday Toll -
All the Screams
Of Earth's Dead
Shall Rise
From Their Lowly Coffined Depths -
With a Mighty Cacophony
And Send Chills of Fear
Down Every Man's Tingling Spine
Come!
Clasp My Hand!
Join Our Brood
As We Dance
Around the Bonfire
Look into Its Flame and Fire
And Ask the Answer -
To Any Question
It Will Speak
And Burn Its Horrifying Reply -
Into Your Misbegotten Mind -
As the Mists Arise

To Engulf You
With the Blood-Dipped Moon
The Dark Clouds Slide Past -
Obscuring All -
And Also You!!!
Now Follow Me -
And I Will Show You
The Way
Walk into Blissful Oblivion
With Me -
And You Will Fade Away -
Slowly . . .
Down the Twisted Path -
Of No Return . . .
I Am Satan -
Seek from Me
The Answers -
And My Spirits
Will Reply -
Will Guide You -
To the Real Light -
That for Which
Ye Seek
I Will Provide
The Answer.

DREAM WORLD

I Feel as if I'm Living in A
Dream World -
Dream World - -
Dream World - - -
And Reality is only a Myth -
A Slender Thread -
That One Treads Slowly Upon
Because it's So Easy
To Lose Your Way
And Find Yourself in A
Dream World
Which is More Real
Than That Life with Which
We are Living
Day by Day -
And if You Think
Reality is Real -
Then You are Sane
And I am Living
Inside My Head!
But I Live There -
More Than in the Present
For the Escape into A
Dream World
Is More Real Than Just Reality -

For Me -
I Live on Memories -
Of My Past -
When My Present
Is So Clouded . . .
So Torn . . .
So Empty . . .
I Can No Longer -
Face the Outside
Because It Hurts -
And I Have Been
Hurt Far Too Deeply -
And Far Too Much!
So, Rather Than Suffer
I Retreat and Live in My
Dream World -
Dream World - -
Dream World - - -
Take Away My Pain and Hurt -
Make Me Calm . . .
Make Me Forget . . .
The Present -
Realities Engulf and Envelop Me
Take Me Dream World -
I Am Yours!

THE MAN IN THE MIRROR?

See That Indistinct Figure -
In the Mirror?
Who . . . Or What . . . Is It?
It May Be Your Personal Dream Maker -
Or . . . It Might Be a Horrible
And Deformed MONSTER!!!
Poised to Leap Out!
Grab . . . And Devour You!
Or . . . A Terrifying Beast -
From the Nether Regions!
Or . . . A Howling. . . Growling . . . Hairy -
Werewolf!!
With Chilling Blood-Red Eyes!
To Pierce Your Very Soul!!
Or . . . A Baying Hound of Hell -
Exhaling Out of its Nostrils -
Freezing Icy Blasts of Air -
To Freeze Your Blood!
Or . . . Is it Merely the Ghost -
Who Inhabits Your Dreams?
Waiting Eagerly to Scare You to DEATH!!!
To Take You Away -
To the Ebony Spirit World -
In the Darkest Pitch-Black Night -
And Welcome You to Hell!

Whoever . . .
Or Whatever . . .
It Is -
It's on the Other Side -
For Now!
Waiting for You to Decide -
What It Really Is!

Chapter 7

VIETNAM

Vietnam was, perhaps, the most traumatic and mind-altering experience of my life. I continue to struggle with both the mental and physical effects of that war some fifty-three years after returning home. It led me to a deep distrust not only of any government entity but also a disgust for the corrupt politicians and self-interested bureaucrats ubiquitously found at the city, county, state, and federal level. In the 20th century wars, the U.S. government has secretly and surreptitiously experimented with the soldiers who were fighting in each conflict, whether it be Agent Orange in Vietnam or nerve gas exposure in Iraq, etc. Soldiers are the guinea pigs that our politicians send off to bleed, hurt, and die for unseen and dubious reasons, all in the name of the United States of America.

** Previously published in *The Other Side: Mist, Mirrors & Strange Tales*. Phoenix, AZ: Fiesta Publishing, 2022. Used with the author's permission.

PEACE SONG

Oh, Fighters of Peace -
Don't You Give Up!
The War at Hand -
Is about to Blow Up
And No One gives a Damn

Oh, You Fighters of Peace -
Please do Rejoice!
Our Leader has called upon the Police
So as Not to give Us the Freedom of Choice

Oh, Where are We going Now?
I ask You!
Is it to Worship LBJ's Golden Cow?
Oh, What can We Possibly Do?

We Must Resign Ourselves to Fate -
We Have to Sit Around and Wait -
While He Sheds More of Our Blood
And the Golden Cow Keeps Chewing His Cud

Resist! Resist!! My Comrades True!!!
And Fight for What is Right!
Demonstrate! Demonstrate!! I Urge You!
So, Perhaps, LBJ will see the Light

But No! He will Send more Police -
To Club You Down in the Streets -
So You Must Boil in Your Own Grease
And Dirty the Gutters with Your Unclean Feet

Rise Up! Rise Up!! Rise Up!!!
One and All -
Yet the Draft will Grab You up in its Full Cup -
So, Protest the Dastardly Call

Protest! Protest! The Draft's Slavery -
Every Man's Born to Be Free -
To Die like Christ on his Own Calvary -
Or . . . Hang on LBJ's Fake Peace Tree

Peace! Peace!! We Vehemently Cry -
But our Echoes just Bounce off the Sky
And the Fucking Draft Keeps Rolling Along
As I Sing This Protest Song

Young People of America Unite!
Wake Up and Join the Fight!
Throw Out the Texas Tyrant -
And let it be a Joyous Event!

Abolish the Draft's Servitude
And End This Criminal War!
Far Too Many Have Already Died -
While Few in the Government have Cried

My Life in Reflection

You have No Say in U.S. Politics -
You Might as Well Be Playing Pick-Up Sticks!
Sit Back and for Your Country Die!
And Forget to Raise the Battle Cry

There is No Hope for Us My Friends -
We can't Even Write our Congressmen!
So - Go Fall under the Police Club -
And Hope LBJ Will Flub

But . . . Just Remember This Tale Is True!
Now, There Is No Hope for You!
So, Go On - Submit to the Draft's Servitude -
And Forget All Freedom's Attitudes.

Twenty-seven months after I wrote this protest song/poem, I found myself in Vietnam as a Combat Rifleman and later as a Combat Medic.

A BIRTHDAY ODE

Who Can Behold the Wonders of Our World
When Man His Fingers around the Moon Curled
And He Set Foot upon That Celestial Body
While My Dad, in Peace, Sat Back and Drank -
His Hot Toddy
We Can Fly to the Moon -
Yet, Our Artillery Still Makes a Loud Boom!
And G.I.s Cry -
While Buddies Die!
Yet, God Wants Us All To Be Happy
So, Therefore I Send This Greeting to My Pappy -
I'm Proud To Be Your Son -
In Nam - My Job Is Almost Done
I'm Thinking of You in Your Best
While Scorning Those Who Protest -
And in This Jungle Hell - If I May -
I Just Want to Take Time to Say -
May You have a very Happy Birthday!
Take Best of Care -
I Wish I were There -
To Help You Celebrate -
And Cut Your Sixty-Odd Candled Cake.

This poem was written while I was stationed in Vietnam. I sent it to my father on his 64th birthday (11/11/1969).

REMEMBRANCES

Over the Mountain and Down to the Sea
Across the Ocean in the Freedom Bird
Came the G.I.
To Fight! To Live!! To Die!!!
All in the Name of Liberty -
When his Time has Come
He knows his Year is Done
And He Remembers the Many Scenes
That He in Sadness, Sorrow, and Joy has Seen
It's a Year of his Life Gone By
One Which, Upon Remembrance, Didn't Fly
He Met a Lot of Good Guys
And Something within him Dies
To Remember the Good and the Bad Times
He Shared with a Tie That Binds
He Left Some Good Men Behind -
Please God, He Prays
To Their Souls be Kind
It's the Little Day-to-Day Experiences
That Pass Through All Men's Consciences
That He Remembers Best of All
With All the Guys - Some Who Got the Call
He Smiles and Remembers the Small Red Mailbags -
That Somehow, Despite All the Snags,
Got Delivered by the Huey Gunships

Without Crashing and Cashing Their Chips
A Letter - - The MOST Precious Thing He Could Get
A Letter from Home over Which He had to Fret
Some of Those back in "The World"
With Their American Flags Unfurled
Wrote the Whole Year Long -
While Others had Forsaken Him and Gone
Then There was the Shared Canteen Cup
Of Hot Cocoa-Coffee to Perk Them Up
After Freezing All Day in the Monsoon Rain
Despite the Outside Temperature of 85°!!!
Which Soaked and Chilled Them All the Same
There was his Heavy Rucksack to Hump
Day after Day through the Jungle Clump
Or the Great C.A.'s Way Up in the Sky
That Brought Him Down to Hear the AK Cry
He Remembers the Work of Doc
And Building Some TOC
On a Dusty . . . Dirty . . . Nameless LZ
Then There's the Medevac PZ
That He Had To Clear
For Wounded Comrades Dear
And There were Always Hundreds of Sandbags To Fill
So Their Bunker Made it Harder for Charley To Kill
The "Mad Minutes" at Three in the Morning
To Stop Those Sappers from Crawling
He Remembers the NEVER Ending Jungle Vines
That Made Him Trip - - - Stumble - - -

My Life in Reflection

And Curse so Many Times -
The Ten-Minute Break taken Alongside a Bomb Crater
Made There by the B-52 Bomb Freighter
Then There were the Claymore Mines
Set Specially to Blow Charley's Mind
And Those Great Fifty-Five Gallon Drums of Fougasse
To Explode in One Beautiful Fiery Mass
He Hated the OP Suicide Squad
And Would Much Rather Prefer the Quad
He Remembers the Cobra Gunships
That Whirled Overhead
As Sweat from his Brow Drips
At his First Baptism of Fire
That Day Every Muscle Did Tire
During Firefights He Remembers -
The Agonized Screams and Shouts
Of the Dying - Of the Living - The Wounded That Mounts
As Precious Minutes Slipped by in a Flash
So That Doc could take a Dash
He put his M-16 on "Rock and Roll"
And let it Take its Human Toll
By Spraying the Area
And When He Gets Back
He'll NEVER Forget the AK Noise -
Crack! Crack!! Crack!!!
Or the Many Times Charley Mortared Him
Making Him Think His Luck was Awful Thin
Later - He Watched Grown Men Cry

Boys No Longer Now - But Men Who Can Die
The Breaks from Battle - - A Two Day R and R
That, Somehow, Charley didn't Mar
There was Always Something to Read
Like The *Stars and Stripes* - A Holy Creed
And God's Padre was There Also
To Help the Grunt Forever on the Go
The Pages of Our New Testaments were Worn
But They gave as Solace in a Life so Torn
He Remembers the Faces of ALL the Dead
Some Calm - Some Painful - Some without A Head
Well, It's Time to go Now
For the Last Time I'll Wipe the Sweat from My Brow
ALL These Things and More I Remember
Memories Bitter, Sweet, True - Like the Last C-4's Ember
Guys Yelling DEROS! ETS!! SHORT!!!
As They Depart Nam's Green Fort
On that Huge Silvery FREEDOM BIRD
They Crowd on Together like an Anxious . . .
Uneasy . . . and Panicked Cattle Herd
It's Time To Go Home -
No More the Jungle will They Roam
In Hell They've Served Their Year
And Back to "The World" They Turn with a Mighty Cheer
They Served Their Country with Distinction
While Others Paid the Ultimate Price -
For Charley's Extinction
'Twas All Done in Freedom's Name

Now, Their Lives will NEVER be the Same
Their Girlfriends - Wives - Mothers are Waiting
So, Let Us Put Aside Our Hating

The FREEDOM BIRD Climbs Swiftly -
For once He can rest Contentedly
He's Homeward Bound
Listening to the Jet's Beautiful Sound
A Smile upon his Battle-Scarred Lips
Now, He Dozes in Peace and Knows
His War is FINALLY Over!

Written in Vietnam, November 1969.

HEROES

The Only People
Who Are Heroes
Are the Dead,
Because We, Who Lived
Are Now in Hell.
There Is No Heaven -
No Peace of Mind
For Us Who Survived
For We Have Indelible
Reprints of the Hell
That We Have Seen.
And Each Day
We Arise To Die
A Little More Within.
The Hopelessness
Of Our Situation
Dulls Our Minds -
Numbs Our Bodies -
Until Nothing Is Left -
And We Flow Onward
Like Wraiths in the Night
Searching for That Happiness
That We Will NEVER Find
Because We're Not Dead Heroes.

CHRISTMAS '69

'Tis Time to Spread the Christmas Cheer
So Break Out That Delicious Cold Beer -
And Sip on Your Eggnog!
Watch the Ol' Man's Chin Droop and Nod
As He Dozes Off Watching the Tube
Ah! Such a Sweet Interlude!
He's Partaken of the Turkey Feast -
And Gloated Himself like a Beast
Now All He Does Is Snore -
A Thing the Grandchildren Adore.
They Long to Climb into the Ol' Man's Lap -
But He'll Awaken with a Snap!
With a Big Ho! Ho!! Ho!!!
And a Smile and a Laugh -
For This Is Christmas Dinner's Aftermath -
The Embers from the Hearth Glow
So, The Old Man Goes to the Vault Below -
And Breaks Out some more *Virginia Gentleman*!
While the O. L. in Church Says Amen -
And comes Home to Burn the Bread - Again!
The Green Tree Droops in Sadness -
This Year's Christmas is without Gladness -
For the Family's separated This Yuletide
And the Ol' Folks This Fact must Abide -
But . . . Let's Not be Sorry . . . or Sad -

'Tis really the Season to be Glad -
Next Year We'll be Together
Sharing the Joy of Cold Christmas Weather -
We'll Down the Eggnog and Then Some
And Decorate the Tree something Awesome -
Perhaps There'll be an Addition - Who Knows?
The Grandchildren will All be Bundled in Clothes -
For the Ol' Man'll take 'Em Sleddin'
Then come Inside to his Favorite Chair's Soft Beddin'
Sip his Drink and Snore Away at the TV Game -
Yes, Then Christmas will Truly be the Same!
So, Merry Christmas to All!
From One Who can't be There at All -
So, I'm Sending You All My Love -
Maybe Next Year We'll See Freedom's White Dove
Peace!

This poem was written in December 1969, while I was in Vietnam. The O.L. refers to my mother (Old Lady). The line, "Perhaps There'll Be an Addition . . ." refers to my girlfriend, A.C., whom I hoped to marry when I returned home from the war. But that joyous occasion was not to happen because PTSD had started to gnaw at the edges of both my post-war life and adjustment to the "normal" world.

OLD MEN YOUNG MEN

The Old Men sit in Their
Comfortably Cushioned Rocking Chairs
And Pleasantly Pass the Days Away -
Remembering Fondly the Times
Of War and Glory
As the Blood Red Sun Slowly Dips
Below the Far Horizon

Young Men are Forced
To Register for the Draft
Praying Their Number
Won't Come Up
Hoping They Won't -
Have to go Off -
To Fight in Some Senseless
Useless . . . Fucked Up . . . War
Started by Their Elders
And Totally Corrupt Politicians
Which is Taking Place -
In some God-Forsaken
Shit Hole of Our World

Old Men sit Behind
Their Fancy Mahogany Desks
Making Decisions -
Concerning Designs and Costs

For the Weapons of Modern Warfare
Not Realizing -
Or Even Remotely Comprehending
The Destructive Power of such Weaponry

Young Men use the Manufactured
Tools of War
That Old Men Have Approved
And Then Die by the Thousands
From Their Use - or Misuse

Old Men Stride down the Long Dark -
Legislative Hallways -
Whispering Hurriedly -
In Hushed Tones -
Making Split-Second Decisions -
Or Compromises
And Then Pass Half-Thought-Out Laws
Along with Useless Spending Programs
Which Affect the Cream of Our Society

Young Men Scream and Cry
Because of Those Hasty Decisions
And, as a Result - DIE!!!
Because Old Men -
Sent Them Off to War
To Old Men -
War is something Glorious -
With Puffed Up Pride
They Remember Their War -

My Life in Reflection

And They Bask in the Sunshine -
Of Half-Remembered Glory -
Forgetting All Too Soon -
The Horrible Price Others Paid!!!
But, They Are Far Too Old -
And Soon . . .
Too Easily . . .
Forget the Price of War's Pain

To Young Men
War Is, Indeed -
As Sherman Said - - - HELL!!!
It Is So Mentally Demanding -
The Images -
So Indelibly Etched -
Stay with You
For the Rest of Your Life -
Especially When -
The Cause Is Not Just -
And the Agony
Of a Shrapnel-Shredded Arm -
Or Its Loss -
Is the Grim Cost!!!

Old Men Shuffle Their Feet
NEVER Paying Much Heed
As to Where They Walk

Young Men Step Lightly
Praying Not to Brush Against -

That Hidden Tripwire
Or That They Don't Step On -
A Bouncing Betty's Trigger -
Or Setting Off an Unexploded
Booby-Trapped Artillery Round!

Old Men Happily Gaze at the Stars -
Recalling the Good Times of Yesteryear -
And Their Innocent Youth
While Wondering About -
Heaven's Black Beauty
When They Marched Off -
To Triumphantly Fight in "The War"

While Young Men
On an Isolated Fire Support Base
Way Out in the Middle
Of the Humid and Fetid Jungle -
Watch as the Flickering Light
From Parachute Flares -
Causes Them to Lose -
Their Precious Night Vision
In the Enveloping Darkness
And They Worry as to Where
Charley might be Crawling
Slipping Silently through Concertina Wire
And Readying His B-40 Rocket
Or Satchel Charge

My Life in Reflection

Old Men Hunt Deer, Ducks, and Quail
NEVER Stopping to Ponder the Pain
The Weapons They Voted For
Might Inflict

Young Men Hunt Other Young Men -
Both with Murder in Their Eyes!
With Cold, Cool Lead
In Their M-16 or AK-47 Rifle Chambers
Which Patiently Waits
For the Trigger Finger
To Release It!
So That the Speeding Bullet
Can Splatter Brains -
Blowing Grey Matter and Bone Chips
All Over the Jungle's Green Vegetation

Old Men Shoot Skeet -
Blasting the Target
Into a Thousand Pieces

As Young Men Endure Artillery Barrages -
And Watch as a Buddy takes a Direct Hit -
And Evaporates – Vanishing into Nowhere
Right before Your Disbelieving Eyes -
So That There Isn't Enough Left -
To Pick Up and Put -
Into a Plastic Body Bag

Old Men Hardly Ever Fight -

Yet, They Revel in sending Young Men
Off to Die in Their Place!

Young Men Fight the Unjust Wars -
So Old Men Can Sleep Peacefully at Night
And Clip Their Coupons in the Morning
In Order to Keep Receiving the Profits -
From the Assembly Line -
Of the Military Industrial Complex!
And Yet, They Make It a Crime for Those
Who Flee to Canada - - - or Elsewhere
And Refuse to Fight an Unjust War

Old Men Trample Through Fields
Taking Their Daily Constitutional
While the Crop of Their Loins
Lies Crying, Dying, in some
Far Off Fucked Up -
Distant and Easily Forgotten Land

Old Men Proudly Salute Old Glory -
Thinking about What a Great Land
It Represents -
But They Don't Actually Care -
If You Please . . . They Say -
Don't Forget to Remit another Dividend -
Generated By -
The Military Industrial Complex
And the Sticky Blood of Young Men

My Life in Reflection

But Young Men
Stare at The Flag and Its Stars
And Remember how It
Betrayed Them

Old Men Recollect How They Fought
For the Great Cause -
To Free Europe from Hitler!
And to Stop the Yellow Pacific Horde!
Young Men Sadly Recall -
They Fought with One Arm
Tied behind Their Back -
Waiting for some Jackass
Motherfucking and Deranged
Battalion Colonel's Permission -
To Return Fire -
After Charley Opened Up on Them
Just across the Rice Paddies
In Front of Them -
From the Nearby "Friendly" Village!!!

Old Men were Greeted -
With Open Arms!
As Liberators!!!
From the Germanic Scourge -
And the Yellow Peril
When They Returned Home -
Victorious!!!

While Young Men Walked Warily -

Into Friendly Villages -
Knowing Full Well -
That Friends by Day -
Were Certainly Enemies by Night

Old Men Hunted Objectives
To Get the Job Done

While Young Men
Fought Hard and Died -
To Take a Patch of Jungle
Then Have to Give It Up -
Only to Return . . .
Next Week . . .
To the Same Spot . . .
And the Next and the Next -
To Senselessly Bleed and Die

As Edwin Starr Sang -
War - What Is It Good For? [4]
It's All the Same Though -
When the Cause Is Not Just -
The Dying Comes Harder!

---

4 Edwin Starr. "War." On album *War and Peace* (1970). Track 1 written by Norman Whitfield and
Barrett Strong.

PLATOON

When I Think of the Dead
I Try Not -
Instead . . . I Close My Eyes -
But Their Young Hardened Faces
Keep Appearing -
Floating Up -
From a Dark -
Sulfur-Smelling and Smoldering
Black Cauldron -
Located in Satan's Red-Hot Furnace
Deep Down in the Burning Bowels of Hell -
Faces -
So Alive . . .
So Dead . . .
Screaming . . .
Why? Why Me?
And Yet I Don't Know -
Not Really -
Why They Died -
Why Their Parents Weep -
At Our Shiny Black Wall -
Thousands of Etched Names
Chiseled into the Black Granite
Stare Back at Us -
Taunting . . . Haunting -

Our Collective Thoughts -
Torturing our Past -
Screaming at our Present!
A Nation's Guilt -
Which No One Can
Quite Wash Clean
A Mass of Bloodied Hands
Writhing!
Reach out to Grab Me
As if to Drag Me Down -
I Helped So Many Live -
I Watched So Many Die -
Their Silent Vacant Eyes -
Now Forever Staring into Eternity -
As Platoons of the Dead -
March off into The Pitch-Black Night -
And the Silent Wind
Now Whistles through the Trees
Swaying the Evergreen Boughs -
Ever so Slightly -
A Common Occurrence -
Just like our Boys -
Our Men -
Who Innocently Marched Off -
To Another War -
And NEVER Returned!!!!
From the Jungle - - or Rice Paddy!
We Weep for Those -

Who Died -
But DO We Really Care?
We, Who Lived in Those Times -
Do -
But Most Others -
DON'T.

FIFTY-THREE YEARS

It's been Fifty-Three Years Since -
I Landed in Vietnam
To Fight an Unjust War
Which America -
In All Its Patriotic Pride -
Would Eventually Lose
At a Horrendous Cost -
Of 57,000+ Lives -
So Many Young Men -
Snuffed Out -
In Their Prime -
Fifty-Three Fucking Long Agonizing Years -
Filled with More Despair -
Than Hope -
I've Suffered Physically -
I've Suffered Emotionally -
A Hole Has Burned through My Psyche -
The PTSD has been an Evil Poison
That Continues to Seep
Throughout My Body -
Oozing Out of All My Pores -
Tainting Me -
Every Goddamned Fucking Day -
And Destroying Relationships -
Vietnam - - -

My Life in Reflection

It did Truly Destroy Me!
And Enabled Me to Ruin -
The Four Lives of Those I Married -
Plus One More Who Was –
For a Brief Moment -
The Light and Love of My Life!
Will They Ever Forgive Me?
I Seriously Doubt It!
Why was I Allowed to Live?
I Guess God wasn't Ready -
To Receive Me -
So . . . Here am I
In My Twilight Years -
A Broken . . . Irreparable Man -
Awaiting . . . No Waiting!
For the Final Shoe to Drop -
To Take Away My Pain -
To Take Away My Angst -
Just . . . Take Me Away -
I've Paid My Penance
In the Hell of This World!
Finally . . . Give Me Some Peace -
Please!

TOO MUCH . . .
TOO MUCH . . . TOO MUCH!!!

I NEVER Quite Recovered -
From Vietnam's Ravages - -
They Still Infect My Mind - - -
Too Much Blood and Guts -
Too Much Lead Slung My Way - -
Too Much Shrapnel - - -
Spinning through the Air at Me!
Wondering How to Duck
Something Hurtling through the Air -
You Can't See It!
You Won't Hear It!!
Until It's Too Late!!!
Then – It Takes a Red-Hot Bite -
And You Live . . . or Die!
Too Much Death -
Not Enough Sleep - -
Living Sleep Deprived - - -
Weary ALL the Fucking Time - - - -
Tired . . . Tired . . . Tired
Always Wondering when Charley
Will Spring his Ambush!
Realizing that It could be Today!
Too Much Heat -
Too Much Rain - -

My Life in Reflection

Too Much Sweat - - -
Too Many Vines
To Cross and Trip Over -
Too Much Weight –
In MY Rucksack!
In MY Medic's Bag!!
85 Pounds!!!
On a 109 Pound Body!!!!
Too Many NVA Mortars and Rockets
Thrown at You -
Causing Unending Worry - -
Day and Night - - -
Is THIS the ONE THAT'S GONNA GET Me?
There was Carnage in Vietnam -
It Followed Me Home -
And It's Perched on My Shoulder
. . . Ever Since For . . .
Far Far Far Too Long!
The Sights and Sounds of Battle
Are Now Dim
Yet They Still Remain!
Too Much . . . Too Much
How Much More of Too Much
Will I Have To Continue to Endure
I Fear - - - -
TOO MUCH!!!!

Chapter 8

DEATH

Wishing for and encountering death has always been one of the major themes of my poetry. From the ages of 15-29, I lived a life where I saw little or no hope in my own personal world. The result was my frustration with living and a desire to end my life. After being both a combat infantryman and medic in Vietnam, where I saw death almost daily, the black shroud of death followed me when I returned home. I suffered (and continue to suffer) from Post-Traumatic Stress Disorder (PTSD), so that the majority of my relationships with women after the war ended badly. What I did not know, but learned in the mid-1970s, was that I suffered from severe depression. This most likely started at an early age and was exacerbated by combat in Vietnam. Thanks to modern day medications and understanding psychiatrists for more than fifty years, I have, for the most part, been able to put both PTSD and depression in abeyance. Yet, they still lurk in the black regions of my inner being, always waiting to emerge.

** Previously published in *The Other Side: Mist, Mirrors & Strange Tales*. Phoenix, AZ: Fiesta Publishing, 2022. Used with the author's permission.

DETERIORATION OF A MAN

Look at Him -
This is a Man
Yes, This **IS** a Man
But, Not for Long
For He Shall Pine -
And Waste Slowly Away -
And Die!!!
Die from That Weed
That Odious Weed!
What Is It?
Tobacco!
You Are Surprised, No?
Look upon This Man Again -
For Fifty Years He Has Taken It -
Fifty Long, Long, Long Years!
Inhaled It -
Now He Coughs - - Incessantly!
Cough! Cough!! Cough!!!
Ah! - All This Is the Work
Of the Evil, Evil Weed!
Slowly, It Takes You
Slowly . . . Slowly . . . Slowly
Slowly Down the Walk of Life
To Death!
Ah, Yes!

This Man Walks Down Those Stairs
One by One
But, His Days are Now Numbered!
A Black, Horrible Shadow Awaits -
Waits for Him at the End of His Walk -
His End will be Quick Now -
Yes! Very – Very Quick!
He Inhales That Poisonous Smoke
Ah! How Good the Taste is to Him!
Ah! How Sweet it Is!
How Wonderful and Soothing it Is!
How Kind!
Yes, Kind!!
Why?
For It Takes His Life!
Every Minute . . . Every Second
Yes, It Does!
But Where Is This Smoke?
Why doesn't it come back Up -
When He Exhales?
It NEVER Will!!!
HA! HA! HA! HA! HA!
Because It Penetrates and Seeps
Into His Lungs!
Yes, Penetrates!
No, it shall NEVER come Up!
He Swallows the Tobacco Smoke
Poor . . . Poor Man!

Yes, Poor Man!
For He has Little Left of his Life
That Horrible Weed Has Taken -
Yes! Has Taken -
Total Possession of Him -
Mind . . . Soul . . . And Body!
He can't live without the Weed!
Yes! Without!
He is Totally Addicted -
It Ruins Him -
The Weed has Him -
Within its Evil Clutches
Oh, Poor, Poor, Poor Man!
He is taking His Own Life -
Yes, Taking It!
Slowly . . . Slowly . . . Slowly
For 50 Years He has been taking It
And, Now He hasn't much Time Left!
Poor Man!
Always with a Weed in His Mouth
We Love Him Dearly -
But He's Going to Die
Yes! Yes! It Is Inevitable
Oh, Damnable Weed
See What you have Done?
Taken the Life of a Good Man -
He was Kind -
He could Teach -

Yes, We will miss Him
Damn You Weed!
Why?
Why do You do This?
You Entice People
With Your Sweetness -
They get Hooked!
You . . . HOOK Them
Oh, When will Someone -
Yes, Someone! Destroy You!
Destroy You as You Have
This Good Man!

I LOOKED UPON A FOREIGN STAR

I Looked upon a Foreign Star
And Wondered just how Far -
Away it would Be
Sitting Up There So High and Free -
And . . . Suddenly a Thought
Passed My Mind -
One of the Complicated Kind
It Seemed to Say
That Man Shall One Day
Try His very Best -
Just like all the Rest
But, No Matter how hard He Tries
He Cannot Break the Light Year's Ties -
NEVER Will He Conquer That Bright Light -
That Shines on Through the Night -
For the Time to get There -
Shall Take Too Long
And Death Shall Sound the Gong.

REFLECTIONS ON DEATH #1

And Out of Darkness
Shall come Man
And in All This Worldly Mess
He will do All He Can

He will find Trouble
That sends All Men to the Depths
And - All That Remains will be a Bubble
For That is all That can be Left

You are Blown into the Winds
To Seek - To Find
Through the Woods and Fens
Of many a Kind
And over the Earth You Shall Rove
Until You Find That Quiet Cove

Come Along with Me -
And Die!
For to be Eternally Free
Is Better Than to Always Fly.

REFLECTIONS ON DEATH #2

And Out of the Blackest Darkness
Shall Emerge That Foul Creature - Man
And on This Dirty World Filled with Chaos
He Will Fight His Way into the Arms of Sweet Death

He Will Always Encounter Trouble
That Sends All Men to the Depths of Doom
And All That Remains of Him
Is Dust
For That is All That should be Left
In the End

Man is Blown by the Winds of Eternal Time
To Seek, To Find – That Wonderful End
Throughout All the Woods and Fens
And over the Barren Earth is He Destined to Rove
Until He finds That Quiet Cove
Where Death Lies Waiting
To Warmly Welcome Him

Come along with Me
And We shall Hunt for Death
Until We Embrace Him in Our Arms -
. . . And Die
For, it is Better for Us to be Eternally Free
Than to Stumble Blindly through a Horrible Life
Which Is Forever Useless . . .

I SAW DEATH WALKING DOWN THE STREET

I Saw Death Walking Down the Street
And I Cried Out to Him,
But He Continued Onward.
I Ran and Caught Up to Him
And We Walked Hand in Hand
Down the Street of Chaos.
I Stumbled over the Trash Bins,
So, I Kicked the Garbage Cans
Out of My Way
But We Kept On.
Fire Raged All Around Us
And Buildings Tumbled Down.
The Wind Blew Hard Against Us
But I Kept Pace.
The Snow Was Deep and Cold
Yet, We Trudged Slowly Onward.
Not A Word Did He Speak
And I Was Content.
We Climbed the Hill
And Watched the Filthy Gutters Overflow.
The Sun Beat Down upon Us,
But I Kept Pace with Him.
He Moved a Little Slower Now,
So, I, Too, Slowed My Pace.

He Seemed To Hesitate
As We Reached the Top.
I Reached Out My Hand,
But He Flung It Back.
We Neared the End of the Street
And He Stopped -
Turned and Pointed,
And I Looked Back.
Floods of Joy Overcame Me
As I Realized What I Had Seen.
There Was Beauty in That Chaotic Mess,
And I Turned to Tell Him So.
But He Was Gone.

Of all the poetry I have written, this poem is my favorite. It was written in 1965 a few days after my 20th birthday during my freshman semester at Texas Christian University.

THE FIELDS OF DEATH #2

I See the Fresh Green Fields of Death -
As I Smell Their Scent in the Cool Morning Air
I Can Taste the Bitterly Cold Food of Death
As I Devour It in the Warm Fields.

There Is No Tomorrow for Me -
Only a Dull, Empty Bucket -
Filled Full of Sorrow
Where is the Good in Life?
Where can it be Found?
Gone are the Living
Scattered Away
Into the Green Fields of Death -
NEVER Again to be Grasped.

All the Land Lies Barren before Me
Deserted and Desolate
The Cooling Wind Sweeps Briskly O'er the Sands
And Washes Away the Precious Blood of Life
And You, My Friend, Are Left -
Alone – Untouched
In the Sun Burnt Fields

Abandoned . . . Forgotten . . . Extinguished
Death Smoothly Whisks Away Your Misery
Into the Fields of Life Unending -
The Quiet Fields of Lethe and Nothingness.

Away! Away!! Away!!! My Friend
Awake and Meet Thy True End - -
The Wonderful Fields of Death
The Sweet Smell of It -
The Bitter Taste of It -
As It Welcomes You Into
Its Loving Arms.

THE LAST FEW MINUTES

The Night Moon was Shining Softly
As the Silver Threads Floated Down -
Down Through the Treetops -
Down Through the Leaves -
And Touched upon My Ground.
My Arm Rests on Cold Pine Needles
While I Listened for the Owl
But, Far Off in the Distance
I Hear a Lonesome Dog Howl
With a Sad and Solemn Bay
It Shattered the Night -
With Electric Tenseness
Halting the Harmonic Cacophony
Of the Locusts and Crickets!
All was Still -
So Deathly Still!
A Pale Cloud Slipped across the Moon
Shrouding It in Dusky Blackness -
Time Stood Still -
My Heart Beat Loudly
Somewhere - Nearby - Water Dripped
The Only Sound to Now Be Heard
The Wind Shifted through the Trees
And Brought an Evil Chill
To My Already Numb Body

Again! That Baleful Howl -
This Time Closer!!!
Perhaps . . . The Beast Senses Me?
Well, It won't be Long Now -
Before - -
Before What?
Before He finds Me!
Then Loud will be his Mournful Howl!
Loud! Loud!! Loud!!!
Loud to the Treetops!
Loud to the Town Below!
And They will come to Search
And Bear Me Up.
The Tree Branches Rustle Now
Back and Forth -
While the Clouded Moon
Is Now Blotted from my Sight
The Water Drips -
More and More!!!
It Drips Thunderously by My Ear -
Because . . . Instead of Water
It Is My Blood That Drips!
Louder and Louder it becomes
Until I Can't Stand It!!

Again - That Fiendish Satanic Howl
So Near! So Near!! So Near!!!
But, O So Far -
Something Cold Nudges My Fingers

And I Open My Heavy Laden Eyes
It is but Only My Dog!
I Smile!
Now a Tear -
As I Stroke Him
One Last Time -
And Then the Blackness
Descends and is Joined
By His Woeful Cry.

MY LAST DAY

Now, at Last, My Day is Finished -
I Have Run My Last Race -
There Is No More Running -
Let the Crowds Clap
Their Last Applause!
For - Let This Final Act Be -
The Be All -
And End All -
Of My Tortured Life -
I Can Travel No Further -
The Sleep of Death
Can Be Much More Sweet
Than the Constant Hell
I Have Faced Here on Earth -
Let There Be No Mourning
By My Bier -
For I Have Surely Gone
To a Far Far Better Life -
Than I Have Found Here on Earth
So Long World -
FUCK You!!!

COME MEET HIM

The Gray Clouds of Eternal Time
Inched Slowly across the Wine-Red Sky,
As Bats Flew from Their Caves
While the Wind Swept Briskly through the Trees
Which, in Turn, Swayed with the Soothing Breeze.
Dark Shadows Moved Silently O'er the Fields
While Tree Branches Clawed Violently at the Sky.
The Sickly Yellow Moon - Half-Hidden by a Cloud,
Seemed to be Wrapped in an Inky Black Shroud.
The Wind Howled! Screamed!! And Moaned!!!
As It Swept over the Now Darkened Land
Heralding the Approach of Something Dark.
Lightning Cracked Off in the Distance
To Be Followed by the Clapping Hands of Thunder
Which Rolled On and On -
From Cloud to Cloud -
Nearer and Nearer to My Place of Hiding.
Rumbling Closer Now
The Thunder Trumpeted the Approach
Of the Bone-Chilling Rain
Which Slammed like Bullets into the Ground,
And, I Realized His Approach was Near -
And No More was Anything Dear to Me.
The Wind's Tempest Tore at My Clothes
As It Screamed Past Me.

The Rain Pounded Me into the Ground,
And I was Numbed.
Suddenly - the Storm was Gone.
I could Hear the Raindrops Dripping off the Branches
As the Clouds Grew Darker and Darker,
I Now Sensed the Approach of Some Mysterious Entity.
It Moved Silently through the Trees and over the Fields
To Come and Take Me to a Better World,
So, Finally, I Can Leave This One Happier -
Ready for the New and Wonderful Life of Death.
My Life in Hell Is Over Now,
And This Heaven That Death offers is Sweet
Compared to This Life of Depression and Frustration.
My Restfulness was Over,
Now No More would I Wander.
As Death Will Forever Be at My Side
To Guide Me Eternally in His Wonderful World
Alone in Life Then as am I Now at Home
In the Arms of Death.

GLASS AND LIFE

What is Life?
It is like a Piece of Glass -
Once You Shatter It -
You can NEVER
Put All the Pieces
Back Together Again!
And you can NEVER
Put Yourself Together -
Again . . .
Nothing is Ever the Same -
That Solid Piece of Glass
Is Now Forever Gone -
And so is your Sanity!
You can't Pick Up -
The Pieces
Because You'll NEVER
Fit All of Them Together -
Again . . .
So When Your Glass
Is Shattered
Forget Life -
It isn't Worth It!
Better to Die -
Than be a Cracked
Piece of Glass

I Wish I were Dead -
Because I Certainly
Can't stand Being
A Broken and Trodden Upon
Piece of Glass
Lying on the Pavement
Where Every Passerby
Steps On and Crushes Me
And Breaks Me -
A Little More
Each Time
Soon . . . I'll Be -
Nothing!
Better Death -
Than This.

DEATH ISN'T PICKY

Death Isn't Picky
He isn't going To Wait Around -
For You to Make Up Your Mind
When YOU want to Go -
Instead . . . He Strikes!
Sometimes Mercifully . . .
Sometimes Unexpectedly . . .
Leaving You There -
With a Lump in Your Throat
Over the Sudden Loss
Of a Friend . . .
A Loved One . . .
Or a Stranger . . .
One Moment You're Here -
And the Next – GONE!
Like Some Ancient Sacrificial Rites
He Gathers His Victims
And Slaughters Them -
Or Sometimes He Comes -
Creeping in to Steal away His Victim
Before You Even Notice It -
While Others - - Preferring Not to Wait -
Welcome Him with Open Suicidal Arms
Yes . . . We ALL have A
Rendezvous with Death!

He's Coming!!!
And Nothing, You, or I, Can Do
Will Stop His Inevitable March -
We May Even Hasten His Arrival
By Stupid Daredevilish Acts
But Mainly, We Try to Run
For as Long as We Can -
Before He Grabs Us!
Pulls Us Up Short!!
And Takes US!!!
How Will it be for You?
Will You Run To – or Away – From Him?

POISON

I Am Poison -
There Is That Certain Something -
Deep Inside Me
Which Turns Them Away -
I Creep in Silently -
And Insidiously!
Not Even I Know -
What it Is
That Turns Them Off
Only - - - That it is My Poison!

Flowing Through My Veins -
Flowing Through My Mind -
The Poison Silently Escapes -
Oozing Out!
It Poisons Their Minds -
And Slowly I Become -
A MONSTER!!!
No matter how Wonderful
Our Relationship Is -
It soon Turns Sour -
And the Girl Leaves Me!

I have often Wondered
What it is about Me -
That Poisons the Minds

Of the Women I Know?

Everything is Nice and Smooth -
And Then, ever so Slowly,
The Poison begins to Creep In -
And Kills Our Relationship -
Slowly Strangling It
Until the Girl Abandons Me!

I Am Vomited Out -
Of Her Life
For Good!!!
And Lie There Hopelessly -

So, Ladies -
Step Lightly and do not Become
Entangled with Me
For, No Matter how Much
You Like . . . or Love . . . Me
I Will - - For some Unknown Reason
Eventually Infect You
With My Evil!
And the Poison will begin to Flow -
Through Your Veins
Until You Realize -
How Hopeless I Am
To Obtain -
Do Not Allow the Poison
To Creep In!
Recognize It!!

My Life in Reflection

Stop It!!!
And Kill the Hope of Love -
Before It Grows

Spit Me Out!
Abandon Me!
Let Me Poison Myself
And Poison .
And Poison . .
And Poison . . .
Until I Am
No More

For Only in Dying
Can My Poison
Be Stopped -
For Only in Death -
Can I Finally Find -
That Sweet Happiness

So, Ladies -
Let Not My Poison
Affect You
Instead - - Permit My Poison
To Poison Me
And End This Misery
Called Life!

NO HOPE #2

There is No Hope
When Hope is Gone -
Only the Despair
Of Living
In a Life Of -
Nothingness!
And All Our Tomorrows
Are like Faded Ghosts
On Their Way -
To a Dusty Death [5]
Without Anyone
To Show Them -
The Way
Could it Be
That This Thing
Called Life
Is Not Really
Worth It?

---

5 Hudson, Rev. H. N., A.M. *The Works of Shakespeare - Vol. 4.* Cambridge [Great Britain]: John Wilson and Son, 1881, 336.
With apologies to William Shakespeare for taking his words out of context. This paraphrase is from *MacBeth* - Act 5, Scene 5, Lines 20-21.

SUICIDE

I Took a Pistol
And Put It
To My Head -
And Just for Fun -
Blew My Brains Dead
So, Now I Lie -
In a Puddle of Blood -
For Those
Who Thought They Cared -
To See

But, There Really
Isn't Much to See
When Someone Dies -
It's All Over Then
The Agony Suffered in Life
Is Over .
Is Dead . .
Is FINAL . . .
And the Peace Beyond
Is Much Better
Than the Hell here on Earth

I Really Wouldn't
Have Done It -
You Know?

Had There Been
A Little More Caring -
A Little More Understanding - -
A Little More Love - - -

Looking at Those
Three Vital Ingredients -
Caring . . . Understanding . . . Love . . .
I was Thrust upon the World -
And When I Met Them
I Couldn't Comprehend
Why They Eluded Me -
So I Rejected Them!
So I Spurned Them!!
My Rejection
Found Nothing -
But Unhappiness
At Not Understanding
Why I Rejected
What I Most Needed?

To See Me in Life
Was to See the Mask -
The Façade -
And Inside -
Was My Self-Erected Wall -
A Shell against the Invaders -
Something I could Crawl
Back Into

My Life in Reflection

And Every Wound -
Every Hurt -
Made Me Scramble
A Little Further
Back into My Cave
Until I Could
Go No More

And When There Was
No Place to Go -
I Made My Choice -
And Gave That Decision -
A THUNDERING Voice!!!

I Am Sure
I NEVER Really Understood
Why
I Pulled the Trigger . . .
And Those around Me
Will NEVER Know
That They Did It –
To Me!
For, I Am Sure -
I Do Know -
There is a Far Far
Better World
Over There
Than That Which
I Have Lived In –

PEACE!
BOOM!!!

THE SEASON OF DEATH

It is the Season of Death -
Just Look at the Trees
And the Leaves Turning
Into Brilliant Colors!
Falling . . . Dying -
As They Lifelessly Drift
To the Hard Ground Below
To Settle and Be Crushed -
Trodden Upon -
By some Heavy Foot
And Now Winter's Deadly Chill -
And Freezing Grip -
Is in the Air -
Killing Off . . . Choking Life -
Bit by Bit -
Until the Cold Gusts
Of the Siberian Express
Sweep Down
Upon All Living Things
To Chill -
To Freeze - -
To Immobilize - - -
And Squeeze Out the Breath
Of Life Its Very Self!
Now Is the Time

For the Old Ones to Die -
To Pass On -
For Winter is Especially Cruel -
And Ruthlessly Picks Her Victims -
Sweeping Them up by the Thousands
And Sending Them Back -
Into the Cold and Frozen Earth
From Whence They Came
It is a Time of Beauty
When Nature's Colors are Spread
Wide as a Peacock's Feathers -
But . . . All This is just a Vile Trick
To Lure Her Victims
Into a False Sense of Security -
And Fall's Early Frosts
Should Provide Ample Warning
That Something is Now Amiss -
If only We weren't so Blind
Soon Winter's Snows Will Descend
To Blind One -
With Their Brilliant White Beauty -
And Grab You
With Their Unsuspecting Cold -
To Swallow and Digest You -
And Freeze You!!!

'Tis the Season of Death -
It is a Dying Time!

THE CANDLE

I am like a Candle -
Slowly Burning Myself Out
Dripping Steadily Away
Until -
Nothing is Left -
Except the Melted Wax -
And Burned-Out Wick
Lying Crumpled and Drained
On the Table
Waiting to be Swept Up -
And Thrown Away -
Now That My Task is Done.

LEGIONS

Legions of the Dead
Follow Me -
Yet . . . How I Became Their Leader -
I Do Not Know
Their Hollow Eye Sockets
And Rotting Purifying Flesh
Nauseate Me
March! March!! March!!!
Onward They Tramp -
Mile after Endless Mile -
A Sea of Dead -
Files Secretly Past -
My Review Stand -
Bloody Red Mouths
Hang Open in Silent Horror -
What They Are Saying
I Cannot Hear -
A Foul Breathed Wind
Causes Tears to Streak Down
Their Ashy Gray Faces -
While Hungry Wolves Howl -
With Salivating Glee -
In the Far Distance -
Anticipating a Dead and Rotting
Fleshy Human Feast -

My Life in Reflection

Is This Armageddon?
No - - That is Over -
The Dark Lord Now Rules!
I Have Won!
And God is Vanquished!
The Multitudes of Dead Soldiers -
Form Up in Silence -
Row after Endless Row -
Disappearing Off into . . . Eternity -
And They Now Stand Before Me -
Swaying in Rhythmical Unison -
I Pick Up the Writhing Serpent
And Point to the Darkened Clouds
Above My Head -
Lightning Dances
At My Bidding
And I Wave My Arms
At the Pitch-Black Sea -
Lapping against the Shore -
Behind Me -
I Watch as the Brackish Murky Waters
Part and Bow before Me!
Pointing to the Earth Between
My Feet
Which Then Splits and Oozes Out
A Bright Volcanic Lava!
Raising My Knobbed Cudgel -
The Wind Quiets

And the Hungry Wolves
Fall Mute -
Hear My Words Minions!
I Now Rule Over You!
The Magnitude Bears Me Up -
Carrying Me on Their
Flesh Rotting Shoulders -
I Am One with Them!
I Am Their Overlord!!
I Am Their Suzerain!!!
Their Power Is Now Mine!
For I Command -
The Legions of the Dead!!!
But . . . Is That What
I Really Wanted?

A KNIFE AND BLOOD

A Dark and Bloody Knife
Tears at My Broken Soul!
Skewers It!!
Rips Me Apart!!!
And My Life Gases
Flow Out from My Body -
Escaping with a Hiss
As the Red Blood Bubbles Burst
Upon Reaching the Cool Outside Air -
The Night is for Loneliness
And I Am a Prisoner -
Of the Night!
Because Night is the Time -
For Dying!
And We All Must Die . . .
Sometime -
A Bloody Hand
Is Upon My Soul
It Rips My Heart Out -
And Destroys Me -
Swallows Me!
Engulfs Me!!
Entraps My Very Being!!!
Grinding Me . . . Into Nothingness!!!!
I Am Life -

I Am Death - -
I Am Dying - - -
I Am Dead - - - -
The Darkness Surrounds Me -
Comforts Me!
Makes Me Realize -
I Am Truly Alone -
All Alone!
Black! Black!! Black!!!
Cold! Cold!! Cold!!!
My Ichor Flows Out -
Turns Black as Foul Sooty Coal -
When It Hits the Air!
And I Float -
Rising above My Body
Looking Down at Death -
It Is Time -
Soon! Soon!! Soon!!!
Can You Hear Them?
They're Coming!
Satan's Legions?
Or God's Angels?
I Know Not -
I Am Past Knowing - - -
I Am Dying - - -
There Is No Pain -
In the Arms of Death!
Only a Sweet Mystic Feeling -

My Life in Reflection

Of Peacefulness
As I Am Taken Up -
All Alone -
There Is No One Else
Born Alone -
We Die Alone -
There Is No One -
But Ourselves to Help Us -
Through That Dark
And Forbidding Door
We Die and No One Cares -
No One Really Cares!
No One Really Cares!!
Not a Soul Cares!!!
That Is How It Is -
And the Horror of Life
Is Soon Joined with That -
Of Sweet Death
And Our Yesterdays -
Are Now Gone -
And We Are Left -
Out in the Cold -
To Live Alone -
To Die Alone - -
Without Anyone - - -
No One!
Not Even Someone
To Care . . . Cry . . . or Mourn

Our Passing!
There Is No Such Thing -
As Love -
It Is Only a Dream -
Ephemeral
Time to Close Our Eyes
And Accept the Peace -
Of Death -
Of Loneliness - -
Of Emptiness - - -
For That Is What Life -
Is Really About!
Life Ebbs
And Sucks Out Our -
Very Marrow -
Emptying This Husk -
Of Flesh -
In This Body - -
We Call Life - - -
Now the Inky Blackness
Descends and Grips Me!
Possesses Me!!
Seizes Me!!!
And My Life Flows Out.

DEATH STALKS ME

I Have This Sixth Sense
That Death Is Stalking Me -
He's Just Around the Corner -
Waiting to Plunge a Knife -
Into My Soul!
I'm Walking Toward Him -
There Is Nothing Else I Can Do!
It's Inevitable -
He's There -
Waiting!
A Horrid Foul Blackness
Has Descended over Me -
Like a Spider's Web -
It Settles Down -
Upon My Shoulders
Dragging Me Downward -
Pulling Me - -
Crushing Me - - -
Smothering Me - - - -
Until There Is Nothing Else -
But Inky Darkness -
Like Gangrene -
Death Attacks My Body -
It Slowly Eats Its Way Towards
My Heart -

Inch by Excruciating Inch
It Feasts on Me!
And Bit by Bit My Body
Is Consumed!
I Look Down and See
Nothing but Black Eternity -
Where My Limbs Used to Be -
It Won't Be Long Now -
Death Will Come to Claim Me -
I Guess I'll Go Willingly.

THE TIME BOMB

I Feel as If
There is a Time Bomb
Within Me -
Ticking Away - -
Minute by Minute - - -
Ready to Explode -
ANY SECOND!
And When it Does -
Flying Shrapnel Will Be Sent -
Throughout My Body -
Disabling My Inner Self
What is This Poison
That Creeps Ever So Stealthily -
Into My System?
It's Killing Me Ever So Slowly -
Sucking Away at My Life -
I Know That -
I Have Only a Few
Short Years -
By Then the Voracious Monster -
Will Have Possessed
My Body -
My Mind - -
My Soul - - -
And like a Withered Leaf

I Will Shrivel Up -
Dry Out - -
And Fade Away!
Each Day is like the Last -
I Die Just That Much More
The Time Bomb Has
Emitted its Poison
Which Now Courses -
Throughout My Veins
Delivering the Fatal Hemlock
To My Muscle Fibers -
To My Soul - -
To My Heart - - -
What is This Realm
We Call Life
But Nothing More Than
A Way Station
On Its Slow Descent to Death?
Eternity Waits for Those -
Who Would Embrace It -
And So, **MUST** I
Deliver Myself Up On -
The Sacrificial Altar
To Watch the High Priest
Plunge His Shiny Black Obsidian Knife -
Deep into My Heart!
My Blood - Like the Azure Sea -
Will Ebb and Flow -

Releasing the Pent-Up Poison
Which Will Carry My Life -
Out with the Tide
And Then, the Time Bomb Will
Stop Ticking
FINALLY!!!

I AM GOING

When I'm Ready to Take That Final Trip
Across the River Styx -
Please Don't Prolong My Going -
Give Me Medicine
To Prevent the Excruciating Pain -
Just Make Me Comfortable -
But Don't Use Life Support
To Put Off the Inevitable -
Just to Give Me a Few More Hours -
Or Days.
After All . . . It Is My Life
God Knows I'm Coming
Why Would You Delay My Seeing Him?
Let Me Go . . .
The Boat Is Waiting -
And Charon Grows Restless.

THE ROAD

I Am Walking down a Road
Which Stretches Miles before Me -
In the Far Distance I Can See
A Dark Cloud Slowly Advancing
Towards Me -
It's Going to Sweep over Me Soon
So I Keep Heading for It -
The Road's Surface Changes
From Asphalt -
To Gravel - -
Then Dirt - - -
Still, I Trudge Onward -
As the Darkness Looms Over Me -
Soon It Will Envelop Me -
And I Will Finally Be at Peace
Having Left All the Agony of Life Behind -
When I Finally Emerge from the Dark -
I Won't Be Here in Our World Any More -
It's Been a Good Trip -
But I'm Anxious
To Forge My Way Home -
Wherever That Is?
Because No One Really Knows -
What's on The Other Side -
So, I'm Weary and Tired -

It's My Time to Go -
I'm Ready for the Whirlwind -
To Take Me!
Guess I'll Close My Eyes, Now
For the Last Time.

THE CANYON

I Am Walking in a Canyon -
Deep . . . Deep . . . Down -
The Light Filters down Dimly
From the Overhanging Rim -
Large Sandstone Red-Colored Boulders -
Lie Scattered across My Path -
I Have to Wend My Way
Slowly around Each One —
NEVER Knowing What
Lies on the Other Side of Each -
As I Grope My Way Onward
In the Semi-Darkness
The Dark Is Fast -
Closing in on Me
It's Not Far Now -
From the Place
Where I'll Lie Down and Surrender
I'll Look Up to See the Fading Sun
As Night Approaches -
And the Stars Begin to Glisten -
I'll Finally Be at Peace -
No More Hurt -
No More . . . Nothing - -
No More Torture - - -
Of Living Each Day

Wondering How I Will
Make It to the Next -
I'll Close My Eyes One Last Time -
Take a Deep Breath –
And Pull the Trigger
To Oblivion!
Three Score and Ten Is More than Enough.

INDEX

ALPHABETICAL LIST OF POEMS

** Previously published in *The Other Side: Mist, Mirrors & Strange Tales*. Phoenix, AZ: Fiesta Publishing, 2022. Used with the author's permission.

ACKNOWLEDGMENTS

First, the Author would like to thank his publisher, Julie Castro, who not only published his second book, *Letters from Potsdam: Colonel John S. Wise's Impressions of the 1945 Berlin Conference*, but also published his third, *The Other Side: Mist, Mirrors & Strange Tales*, and now this book of poetry. Every writer needs a cheerleader and not only was Julie incredibly helpful with *My Life in Reflection: 101 Poems of Love, War, Satire & Death*, but she offered a lot of encouragement, which enabled me in the completion of this book. Her suggestions, comments, and ideas made this a much finer poetry tome. Lastly, her faith in me is deeply appreciated.

A special thank you to Stefan Hansen of Creative Instincts for his skill in creating not only the cover for this book, but also the interior design and typesetting. His vision and artistry enhanced this book far beyond what I could have ever imagined. Stefan's design captures the turbulence, despair, and anguish I have experienced throughout most of my life along with an elusive serenity that fleetingly appears in my poetry. The importance of Stefan's enticing design not only brings a book alive but also sets the mood for the reader.

I would also like to give a great big thank you to my proofreader extraordinaire, Ashley Niro. Not only did she do a fabulous job with my previous novel, *The Other Side: Mist, Mirrors & Strange Tales*, but her comments and editing suggestions for this poetry book were most appreciated and spot on.

ABOUT THE AUTHOR

E. Tayloe Wise grew up in Charlottesville, VA. On his mother's side of the family, he is a direct (7th generation) descendant of Martha Dandridge Custis, whose second husband was George Washington. He is the great, great grandson of Virginia Governor Henry A. Wise. He graduated from Texas Christian University with a degree in Geography, Sociology, and Anthropology in May 1968.

The following month, June 1968, he volunteered and enlisted in the U.S. Army and was trained to be a combat infantryman, or in military lingo, an Eleven Bravo, which was the job title code for his Military Operation Specialty (MOS). He arrived in Vietnam on May 2, 1969, and was assigned to serve with the 1st Air Cavalry Division, Air Mobile. While with his infantry company, he operated in the jungles of Tay Ninh Province and saw heavy combat during which he became his platoon's medic. He was awarded the Army Commendation Medal for Heroism along with three Bronze Stars, two of which were for Heroism. He also was awarded the Combat Infantryman's Badge and the Vietnamese Gallantry Cross. He ended his tour as an aide to Major General E. B. Roberts, the Commanding General of the 1st Cav Division and left Vietnam on April 8, 1970, after serving 342 days in country.

He then worked in his family's commercial real estate business in Charlottesville before retiring in 1989. He was accepted into the graduate school at the University of Richmond where he earned a Master's Degree in History in 1991. He did post-graduate work at American University in Washington, D.C. In the late 1990s and the early 2000s, he taught Asian History at the University of Richmond. He has also taught Asian History in Richmond, VA, at The Shepherd's Center and The Osher Center, both Open Universities for seniors.

His book, *Eleven Bravo - A Skytrooper's Memoir of War in Vietnam* was published in 2004 (MacFarland) and is still in print. In addition to his Vietnam book, he has also published both *Letters from Potsdam: Colonel John S. Wise's Impressions of the 1945 Berlin Conference* (Fiesta, 2022), and *The Other Side: Mist, Mirrors & Strange Tales*, (Fiesta, 2022).

Books also by E. Tayloe Wise

The Other Side:
Mist, Mirrors & Strange Tales

Delve into the phenomena of present, past, and outer-dimension adventures

Letters From Potsdam:
Colonel John S. Wise's Impressions of the 1945 Berlin Conference

Letters to Colonel Wise's wife from the editor's father who attended the 1945 Potsdam Conference

Eleven Bravo:
A Skytrooper's Memoir of War in Vietnam

A narrative of the author's 1969-1970 combat tour in Vietnam

www.ingramcontent.com/pod-product-compliance
Lightning Source LLC
Chambersburg PA
CBHW060904120626
46553CB00001B/196